BLYTH TAIT'S
CROSS-COUNTRY CLINIC

BLYTH TAIT'S
CROSS-COUNTRY CLINIC

KENILWORTH PRESS

First published in hardback in 1999 by
Kenilworth Press Ltd, Addington, Buckingham, MK18 2JR

Paperback edition 2004

ISBN 1-872119-74-3

British Library Cataloguing in Publication Data
A catalogue record for this book is available from the British Library.

Layout and typesetting by Kenilworth Press

Printed in Singapore by Stamford Press

Contents

4 PROBLEMS ARISING AT COMPETITIONS

5 TRAINING EXERCISES

Preface

During my teaching clinics, which I conduct throughout the world, I am constantly asked a wide variety of questions related to cross-country riding. This book is a collection of the most frequently encountered problems and offers a number of solutions that I have found to work for me.

Most riders experience jumping difficulties at some stage of their career. Due to varying circumstances, no two problems are exactly the same, but nearly all can be rectified by a greater understanding, coupled with sensible, systematic training.

The first four sections of the book are designed to allow quick reference to specific problem areas. The fifth section gives a range of training exercises which I use at home to solve my own training problems or, if no problem exists, simply to enhance all-round performance. En route the book goes some way to explaining the ideals behind my own training methods. I hope its pages will prove useful to riders, both before problems occur as well as after.

Good luck!

ACKNOWLEDGEMENTS

I would like to make a special point of thanking all the riders who feature in the photos and especially those who have been caught out in an unlucky moment. Since this is something that happens to us all (as evidenced on the front cover) and on a more regular basis than most of us would care to admit, I hope they will forgive me for not showing them in a better light!

PHOTO CREDITS
John Birt, 99; David Fraser, front cover, 41, 45, 86; Horse and Rider, 117; Peter Llewellyn, HorseSource Ltd, 43 (top, both); Bob Langrish, back cover, 37, 71; Nick Morris, 10, 57; Paul Raper-Züllig, HorseSource Ltd, 43 (bottom), 68; Stephen Sparkes and Helen Revington, frontispiece, 3, 11, 14, 15, 16, 22, 24, 26, 28, 29, 32, 34, 36 (both), 38 (both), 39, 49, 51, 55, 56, 58, 59, 61, 63, 64, 66-67 (sequence), 73 (sequence), 75, 76 (both), 77 (both), 79, 81, 82 (sequence), 85, 88, 92 (both), 101, 103, 104, 109, 112, 116; Shaw-Shot, 5.

LINE DRAWINGS
Carole Vincer

1

Horse Problems

RUNNING OUT

Q. What are the probable causes of a run-out?

- The most significant reason is a lack of rider control. The horse, being considerably stronger, must display a submissive attitude to his rider's demands and should not be allowed to dictate matters of speed or direction.

- This lack of control can often be the result of too much speed on the approach, or the horse's frame and stride being too long and disengaged.

- A run-out can also be the result of a concern or suspicion of the obstacle by the horse, particularly with an inexperienced horse being presented to an unusual fence for the first time.

Q. What can I do to prevent a run-out from happening?

- Most importantly, slow down and gain maximum control. A more experienced horse could remain in a slow canter; a green novice may even need to return to trot in order that the rider can influence the direction and speed.

- Collecting and condensing the horse's frame and stride will be useful. This will allow some containment of the horse's energy and impulsion.

- The rider should keep his or her eyes up, trained on the fence ahead. Looking up will make the rider's reaction quicker, looking down will not.

- It will be necessary for the rider to remain a little more upright in his/her upper body position. Do not let the shoulders topple forward on the approach or lose the consistent rein contact. (See 'Dropping the Horse' – page 38.)

Obvious disappointment. A run-out has occurred at this narrow fence on a downhill approach.

Q. What should I do to rectify the problem?

• Always correct the mistake. Just as you would repeat, for example, an incorrect strike-off in your dressage training, a run-out in jumping training must be rectified. Don't give up.

• Try not to simply prescribe a circle in your re-approach. For example, if the horse chooses to run out to the left, first stop him from running on to the left, turn him back towards the fence with the right rein, returning in front of the fence. At this point a mild reprimand could be executed by way

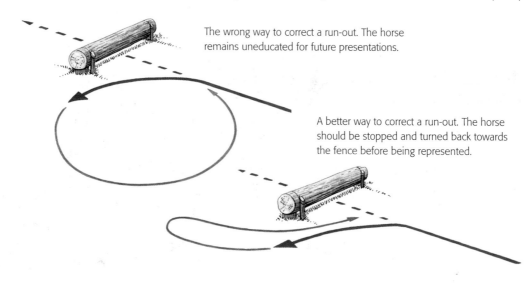

The wrong way to correct a run-out. The horse remains uneducated for future presentations.

A better way to correct a run-out. The horse should be stopped and turned back towards the fence before being represented.

of a growling voice. Having indicated that the horse has disobeyed and that running left is not an option, turn right, reorganise and make another approach. Thus you have not simply continued to turn in a left circle, but have corrected the mistake sensibly, educating the horse in the process.

• Clarity and correction will educate the horse to apply himself, to look for a way over the fence and not a way round it. With this in mind it may be necessary, particularly with a green horse, to erect two guide rails, one on each side of the fence, or just one on the side that he is running out, to channel him over the fence, making running round it more difficult.

• A successful attempt will enable the rider to reward the horse, which will develop confidence, trust and willingness.

• Initially the guide rails can be placed so that one end is resting on the top of the fence or wing and the other on the ground out in front. Then, as the horse becomes more confident, they can be laid directly on the ground, which will still encourage straightness, before being removed completely.

Q. If I make a slow, more controlled approach and the horse refuses, should I be concerned?

• Initially, no. Compared to a run-out, I consider a refusal to be the lesser of the two evils.

A guide pole placed on a training fence will prevent the horse from running out. It is also useful for keeping the horse straight.

- Firstly gain the control required to stay straight, then you can ride more positively forward, perhaps quite strongly to prevent or rectify the stop.

- If the rider has control concerns he will be anticipating a run-out, approaching half-hearted, steering, pulling and kicking at the same time. Clarity is necessary when influencing the horse.

Q. How do I recognise whether my horse is concerned and frightened or just being naughty?

- For the inexperienced rider this is not always easy to gauge and it may be helpful to get the opinion of an experienced eye. Usually with fear or anxiety the run-out will combine an obvious change in rhythm, such as slowing down, spooking or even a dramatic speeding up away from the fence.

- If running-out is associated with concern about the fence then the problem should be addressed with patience. Don't bustle the education.

- If associated with naughtiness, the problem should be rectified in a firm, clear, efficient manner.

- A run-out at a schooling fence at a second approach (after an initial completion) should not be tolerated.

Q. Is there any flatwork that I can do to help?

- As is nearly always the answer with jumping problems, yes.

- Exercises to gain control will help. For example, lots of downward transitions, implementing half-halts, engaging and collecting the horse's stride, and lightening the forehand.

- Educating the horse to step sideways from the leg will further enhance the rider's ability to ride straight or to correct a horse that may be slightly crooked on the approach to a jump. A simple leg-yield, or even more sophisticated lateral work, will help.

- Often with a horse that is lacking balance, an attempt to straighten or turn a horse simply by pulling on the inside rein will be unsuccessful. The horse may turn his head, only to lose his weight out through the opposite shoulder or even resist the strong hand and go against it in the other direction.

LEAD CHANGES

Q. My horse consistently lands on the same canter lead. Should I worry about this?

• For basic jumping and when going straight ahead after the fence, no; but when riding fences off turns, on curves or in a course of fences it will eventually become a problem. If the leading leg happens to be the incorrect one, i.e. the outside leg instead of the inside one, it will hinder riding positively forward towards the next fence in a good balance.

Q. Why does my horse always land on the same leading leg?

• Mostly it is as a result of either stiffness on behalf of the horse or a problem created by the irregular balance of the rider.

• If the horse shows lateral stiffness in his flatwork he will be likely to display stiffness also in his jumping. We must endeavour to make the horse supple and ambidextrous in his training on the flat and also over fences. See Training Exercises – Lead Changes, pages 107-109.

• If the rider leans to one side or the other when jumping he may upset the horse's balance. The rider should stay centred over the horse.

REFUSING

Q. Why does my horse refuse?

• There can be many reasons why a horse will refuse: it might be that he is frightened by either the jump or his rider's bad position; he may be unbalanced in his approach, travelling too fast or even too slow.

Q. How will I know which cause creates my specific problem?

• If you are inexperienced it may not be easy to recognise why your horse is stopping.

• If possible, seek the advice of a more experienced eye.

• First try to rule out all possibilities of discomfort. Ask yourself: Am I jumping the horse on ground that is too hard, for instance? Is he hurting?

This is a young horse being presented to one of his first cross-country obstacles. The fence is fairly straightforward, being of rounded profile, solid and well built. Through inexperience he is unsure of the demands, and refuses. Because the rider is not leaning forward and has his weight well into the stirrup, a spill has been avoided.

Could he be unwilling as a result of badly fitting tack? For example, is his saddle pressing on his withers, or is he over-bitted?

• Then look to yourself as the rider: Am I catching him in the mouth when he jumps? Am I landing heavily on his back? Am I fully committed to succeeding or am I weak and tentative?

Q. When should I be sympathetic and when should I be firm?

• You should be able to recognise when a horse is frightened of a fence. It will usually be associated with spooking, an alteration in rhythm, i.e. a stop-start approach, or even a consistent change of direction off your straight line.

• With a nervous horse you should be sympathetic and unhurried. Do not over-face a horse that is lacking confidence.

• If the horse is being ungenuine, e.g. he is stopping well away from the fence or is stopping on a second approach having already jumped the fence once, then it is time to be firm. Be sure that the horse is responsive to the leg. He must move forward, both on the flat as well as when jumping.

• You may need to introduce your voice and whip, but be equally quick to reward a favourable response.

With sympathetic education the horse is growing in confidence and answering his rider's requests.

Q. How will I know if I am too slow?

• You will simply seem to 'run out of petrol'. It is important that you are riding with sufficient energy and forwardness to make the jumping effort seem easy within the canter rhythm.

• There should be no obvious increased energy burst required for the jump itself.

Q. How will I know if I am too fast?

• Because your refusal will also probably happen quickly – at the very last minute, or even by sliding into the fence.

• Riding too fast will usually create a loss of balance and control as well as accuracy.

Q. What should I do if I have experienced a stop?

• When training, don't let the horse dash away from the jump. Stay momentarily in front of the fence. You will not be eliminated in training.

• The horse should not choose to run away from the problem in panic but should instead face up to the jump and assess it.

• Be sure that it is you who turns the horse away, in your own time.

• Don't go miles away from the jump for a second presentation. Be more positive a second time by staying a little behind the centre of balance to give yourself additional strength. Don't pitch forward with your upper body but remain more upright with your shoulders, keeping a close contact with your seat. Don't lose the horse's balance by abandoning the rein contact on the approach, an action commonly known as 'dropping the horse' – see page 38. Keep the horse confident by riding him with a strong leg into a supporting hand.

RUSHING OR ANTICIPATING

Q. What problems will occur if my horse rushes his fences?

• Basically all the desired principles to ensure a good, clean, correct jump will be lost.

• Loss of control and balance will be obvious, not only on the approach but also at the point of take-off. It is unlikely that the horse will allow the rider to soften his hands and close his leg to encourage a good bascule if he (the horse) is pulling towards the fence excessively. Instead it is likely that the rider will restrain with his hands and remove his lower leg. This in turn

A rushing horse invites the rider to pull on the reins, which will not produce a correct jump. This horse has a severely inverted (hollow) outline.

could result in resistance on the approach, with the horse inverting (hollowing) or leaning on the bit.

Q. What could be causing my horse to rush?

• Most likely it will be a psychological reaction to jumping, although any serious physical defects in his balance could also contribute. Anxiety, over-enthusiasm, lack of discipline and education can all induce rushing.

Q. How can I stop my horse from rushing?

• Be consistent in your training. Horses respond well to repetitive educa-tion, so always be particular that the horse remains in control and is balanced.

• Ride in a regular rhythm to your fences. Try not to alter the speed dramatically, either speeding up or slowing down in the closing few strides.

• Use exercises in gaining control to teach the horse to wait for you. This may include frequently halting the horse on his approach in front of the fence. Give him a pat once he has stopped to encourage relaxation before re-presenting.

• If the horse rushes badly, educate him with small fences, at which it will be easier to control him. At times poles on the ground will be sufficient to give you an indication of the horse's behaviour when jumping.

• Insist on control and a consistent rhythm when passing over a single pole or when trotting small fences.

• Be careful not to anticipate the problem yourself. If you expect the horse to rush then you are unlikely to ride the horse through the problem.

• Don't panic near the fence but simply maintain your rhythm, establish control and allow the fence to come to you.

Q. Are there any particular exercises I could do to prevent my horse from rushing?

• Flatwork exercises that will improve the horse's balance and control will be useful. Downward transitions, the use of half-halts and improving the canter and self-carriage will all help.

• Introduce vee poles (as described in Training Exercises, page 102) to further educate the horse to wait and back off his fences. The vee poles will reduce the need for the rider to pull against the horse on the approach.

● Generally any exercise that increases the horse's rideability will help. For example, riding a straight approach to the fence, then making a circle towards the leading leg close to the fence before proceeding to jump, will encourage the horse to listen and wait rather than rush and anticipate.

Q. Can I approach too slowly?

● Yes. If you restrain the horse excessively you could create a 'tug-of-war' situation, where the horse will want to pull against you for sufficient freedom to negotiate the fence.

● Ride softly forward with enough energy to jump the fence easily. This will give the horse confidence and he won't feel the need to speed up.

ADDING UNWANTED STRIDES BEFORE A FENCE

Q. Why does my horse add small 'getting ready' strides in front of his fences?

● Probably the major cause is that you are approaching the fence with a disengaged canter and the horse is responding by attempting to 'coil his spring' to enable himself to jump off his hocks. If the horse's balance is on his forehand with his hocks trailing, he will lack balance and confidence.

● Alternatively, the approach may be too fast, with the horse decelerating deliberately in order to be able to back off to avoid hitting the jump.

Q. How can I ensure that I take off on an even forward stride?

● Work on the horse's engagement in canter (see Improving the Canter, page 116) to ensure that he has sufficient impulsion. This will enable you to release some of his contained energy in your approach, to lengthen the horse's frame and stride without losing balance.

● Allowing the stride to lengthen by releasing the hand forward will be better than introducing additional leg pressure, where the stride may just get faster.

● Be sure that the horse is not behind your leg. He must remain forward throughout his flatwork without needing constant reminders.

- When training at home construct your schooling fences to encourage forward riding. Bring the ground lines out a little on your upright fences and avoid making your oxers too square. Slightly ascending parallels will soften the profile of the fence, enabling the horse to be more forward through the air.

- Be sure to ride positively forward on landing to encourage no loss of rhythm or impulsion.

- Do not topple forward in your approach and drop your horse onto his forehand.

- Think 'up hill'.

Q. When does adding unwanted strides become critical?

- When riding related lines and combinations, especially when these distances are long.

- It will also be a problem when riding fences that involve greater spreads, such as wide ditches and oxers. Here it will be essential that the stride remains open and that the horse does not become backward and 'chip in'.

SHOOTING AWAY AFTER THE FENCE

Q. Why does my horse suddenly accelerate after jumping?

- It could be a response to an unpleasant experience created by the rider: for example, the rider's weight banging heavily on the horse's back on landing, the rider being left behind the movement, or the rider falling forward, losing control with lengthening reins.

- It may be due to a lack of control or a loss of balance. It will certainly indicate a lack of rhythm.

- It may be as a result of exuberance or enthusiasm, requiring adjustments in training, horse management and attitude.

Q. How can I prevent the problem from happening?

- Firstly, ensure your own balance is independent. Take the impact of

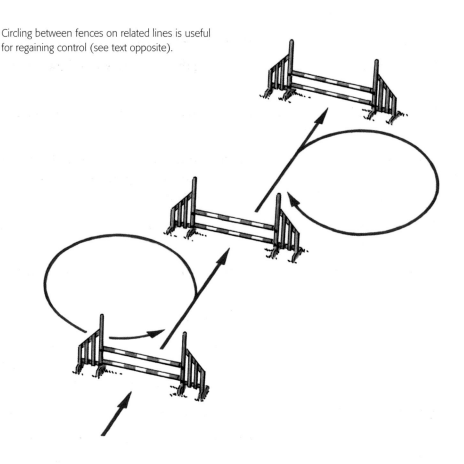

Circling between fences on related lines is useful for regaining control (see text opposite).

landing on the stirrup, don't get left behind the movement or throw your shoulders forward over the jump.

● Pay particular attention to the quality of the canter in the first stride after the jump. Be immediately prepared to gain control. Don't leave the horse on a long rein but instead ensure that the connection between your leg and hand is maintained. The importance of the need to be immediately controlled and balanced after the jump will become increasingly apparent when riding related distances or turns between jumps.

● Make sure that the energy level on the approach to the fence is sufficient for the obstacle itself.

● Being under-energised may result in an increased effort on take-off, making rider independence more difficult.

● Conversely, don't over-energise or you may induce problems with control, rhythm and speed.

Q. If my horse displays this problem how might I rectify it?

• Work on exercises of control, collecting the stride, downward transitions, etc.

• Once certain that the problem is not created by the rider you can educate the horse out of the habit.

• It may be easier initially to regain lost control or increased speed after the fence by bringing the horse back on a circle. Bending the horse's body may assist. Be sure to circle evenly in both directions.

• These circles can be executed in related lines between jumps (see diagram opposite).

• Eventually you should be able to regain control on a straight line, execute a downward transition or even halt.

• Take your time; be unhurried when eradicating this problem.

• In extreme cases, I would even rein-back the horse after halting to further clarify the message that he should not fall forward in his balance but should wait and listen. He must not take charge but must be submissive.

• Remember to reward a favourable response.

• In dire cases, when attempting to stop on a straight line it may be necessary to make use of, say, an arena wall if indoors, or a very high surrounding fence. Take care not to present the horse to anything it might mistake for a jumpable obstacle.

• Start the re-education over very small fences or even just poles on the ground. This will increase the rider's chances of an independent seat and enable a decrease in the energy level required, so placing the rider in a position of greater effectiveness.

JUMPING INVERTED (HOLLOW)

Q. Why does my horse jump inverted?

• An inverted jumping technique, where the horse negotiates an obstacle with his head high, back hollow and lower limbs down, is usually the result of resistance to excessive restraint from the rider, either during the approach or over the jump itself. Possibly the greatest cause of resistance is

This photo illustrates a fence taken at speed. It would be preferable for the horse to be showing more roundness over the jump and less resistance.

restriction. Be sure not to create a barrier that the horse can work against.

• Incorrect early education can establish bad technique during a horse's formative stages and this can be very difficult to correct, even by an experienced rider.

• If the horse is afraid to take the contact forward during his jump because he has been constantly caught in the mouth by his rider, he will be reluctant to lower his head over the fence. The lowering of the head and neck when jumping enables the horse to raise his shoulders and forearms and round his back.

Q. Can an inverted jump cause other problems?

• It will increase the probability of a careless technique. If the horse's head and neck are upright the legs will more than likely be down as a counterbalance.

• It will be difficult for the horse to jump cleanly from a deep take-off point and will result in the need for the horse to stand off his fences.

• An inverted jump will be less easy for a rider to sit comfortably on. A more rounded, softer technique will permit greater rider security.

- A horse that shows tendencies to jump inside out at ordinary fences will inevitably find fences requiring greater athleticism difficult. Fences such as bounces, drops, coffins, etc. require good use of the neck and back.

Q. How can I improve my horse's inverted jump?

- Any exercises that improve the horse's elasticity, softness and roundness, whether in flatwork or jumping, will be valuable.

- On the flat I would encourage the horse to stretch forward and down, loosening his back and freeing his shoulders. Do this by engaging the hindquarters to promote a little more weight in the rein, which may then be eased forward to extend the frame and stride.

- The use of gridwork, gymnastic jumping and lines of fences should be adopted. The benefit of jumping grids is that a soft, forward rhythm can be established with reduced dependence on the rider's hand for the maintenance of balance. Once into a grid or related line (gridwork usually involves one or two strides between fences; related lines could be four or five strides) a generous crest release (where the rider eases his hand forward along the horse's neck to allow freedom) can be offered if the fences are placed on true distances. The rider should encourage the horse forward with the leg to a deep take-off point to influence the extent to which the horse is required to raise his shoulders and legs quickly to jump the fence cleanly.

- Canter poles can be placed before take-off, at approximately 9–11 feet (2.7–3.3m), to draw the horse in deep. A pole could also be put down on the landing side at the same distance to entice the horse to look down. Lowering his head will discourage hollowness and improve his bascule.

DRIFTING

Q. Why does my horse drift sideways when he jumps?

- Drifting sideways when jumping is usually a result of stiffness or a lack of suppleness. As the horse shows a reluctance to draw his weight onto his hindquarters and then execute his jump through the use of a softened back, he will look for an alternative method of clearing the obstacle.

- Moving sideways enables the horse to be less athletic, allowing him more time to be slower with his jumping technique.

This horse is drifting off line. Notice how the rider is already looking towards the centre of the next fence. This will permit a more immediate correction of the problem.

Q. Will drifting create further problems?

• Yes. It could lead to greater problems when riding straight lines and combinations. Severe drifting might eventually cause a run-out at narrow obstacles such as arrowheads and corners.

• Drifting could also affect the efficiency of turns before and after the jumps and if left unattended, stiffness and a lack of suppleness could in time spoil the horse's overall technique.

Q. Could I be contributing to my horse's drifting?

• A drifting horse could certainly be the product of bad riding. An obvious crookedness in position or unbalancing effect from a rider, exaggerated leaning off centre when jumping, could easily contribute to a sideways movement. The horse might attempt to counterbalance his rider's inadequacies.

• Try to sit straight in the saddle with equal weight in each stirrup. Keeping your eyes up and ahead will alert you to any sideways motion.

Q. What exercises will help remedy the problem?

• Basic flatwork exercises to improve suppleness, such as leg-yield, lateral work and bending, will help. Educating the horse to step sideways in response to the application of your leg will make the horse easier to adjust and make straight.

• Simply using the reins to correct crookedness might have the effect of turning the horse on the approach or in the air. It could also have an adverse effect on the horse's bascule, by increased restriction.

• If the correction can mainly be achieved from the leg, forward flow and rhythm can be maintained.

• The use of guide poles to offset a sideways drift will initially act as prevention and, long term, could act to improve or correct the problem.

BACKING OFF

Q. Why does my horse 'back off' his fences so excessively?

• Usually the horse will back off his fences as a result of some kind of concern. He may be nervous of the fence itself or he may be generally lacking confidence and trust. Other causes could be that he is experiencing discomfort, exhibiting signs of being over-faced or is simply displaying unwillingness.

• Try to determine which cause might be applicable to your horse. Has he had a confidence knock recently? Are you rushing his development? Or are you jumping too frequently on firm ground?

Q. Could I be contributing to my horse backing off?

• Quite possibly, if you are being weak in your own attitude and approach. Be sure not to look down into the bottom of your jumps but instead look up and ahead to encourage more positive forward riding.

• Be light in your seat. Don't sit heavily in the saddle or get behind the horse's movement.

• Ensure that you are being effective in the use of your lower leg. Do not compensate for a weak leg by pushing with your seat, which will probably only have an adverse effect.

Contrary to the rider's endeavours, this horse is backing off his fence more than is good for him. In this frame, with his nose too far in front, he could lack the necessary impulsion and power to successfully negotiate the fence.

• Make sure that you are secure in your own independence of balance during the jump. Any rider insecurity such as catching the horse in the mouth will punish his generosity and could lead to unwillingness.

Q. Can I train to reduce the problem?

• As always, flatwork will help to overcome a jumping problem. Try to develop your most effective, engaged canter to ensure plenty of impulsion (contained energy). The degree to which you will be able to lengthen your horse's stride at any time will be directly related to the amount of initial collection.

• Work to develop a sharp response from your horse to your lower leg. It should not be necessary to constantly remind your horse to remain 'in gear' and show a willingness to move freely forward. In extreme instances you may need to introduce the whip to act as an extension to your leg aids to encourage more respect for your leg.

• Do not over-face your horse in his training. Work at developing his confidence by reducing the heights of your fences. Always construct encouraging fences. False groundlines are not advisable. Use slightly ascending spreads that might help to draw the horse forward in his approach and during the jump as well.

- Use gymnastic exercises and gridwork that encourage forwardness. Start with distances that initially are very comfortable for the horse (not too long). Slowly increase the demands by subtly lengthening the distances once a positive rhythm and confidence are established.

- Remember that when attempting to lengthen your horse's stride you should remain elastic in your arms. Do not fix your hands at the horse's withers and simply apply more leg, as this will only develop faster rather than longer steps.

Q. Will backing off create bigger problems?

- As is nearly always the case, a problem such as this that is left uncorrected will almost certainly lead to greater problems when riding combinations or fences on related strides.

- When tackling cross-country fences that require your horse to be bold and lengthen his stride, he must not back off. Backing off at, for example, a wide ditch with a tall brush behind it, would be most undesirable.

CARELESS TECHNIQUE

Q. Is it possible to improve my horse's carelessness?

- Yes, to an extent. It is possible to encourage a horse to be more careful with training, but it is likely that your competitive career will be more successful if you have a horse that is instinctively careful.

- When selecting a horse for potential performance try to look for immediate natural awareness and a reasonably correct jumping technique.

Q. How can I make my horse more careful?

- First try to identify where the obvious weakness lies. For example, is the horse loose and careless with his front legs? Is he slow and casual with his back legs? Are his hind legs cramped up behind instead of softly trailing?

- Pay attention to his balance as well. Check that he is not leaning on your hand, travelling on his forehand, going too slow or too fast, or being inverted (hollow).

- Once the problems have been highlighted, training methods to improve the specific fault can be introduced (see below).

- For all problems of carelessness it would be advisable to work with substantial, well-constructed jumping equipment. Flimsy, lightweight materials will not encourage respect from the horse.

- Inexperienced horses could even be introduced to solid, natural obstacles early in their education.

- Try to assist the horse in his balance and approach but try not to over-protect him from the jump.

- Place the emphasis mainly on his own self-reliance so he does not come to depend heavily on your own accuracy. The best types of fences will be logs, walls, ditches, etc.

Q. What types of exercise should I use?

- For all-round improvement in self-awareness, polework exercises such as cavaletti and the canter-pole exercises (page 116) should help.

- Small bounces (page 100) and gymnastic grids (pages 113-116) will continue to build athleticism and sharpness. Again, the development of self-reliance should be encouraged with the understanding that care can be nurtured without the need to jump excessive heights.

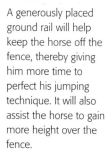

A generously placed ground rail will help keep the horse off the fence, thereby giving him more time to perfect his jumping technique. It will also assist the horse to gain more height over the fence.

• If the jumping technique weakness is focused on the horse's front legs then vee poles exercises (page 102) and diagonal pole on oxer exercises (page 103) could be introduced. Try to ride the horse forward in an energetic, dynamic canter with the stride engaged, rather than allowing the horse to be long and flat in his way of going.

• If the careless technique involves the horse's back legs then attention should be paid to softening the jump, encouraging an accentuated bascule. A useful exercise is described on page 111.

NAPPING

Q. What are the most likely causes of napping?

• Napping is most likely to be an adverse reaction to fear or confusion.

• Normally it is a retaliation against too much pressure being applied during a time of concern or misunderstanding from the horse.

• Eventually some horses learn to use napping as an extreme evasion to submission, displaying much disobedience and stubbornness. But even then

A young horse showing reluctance to approach the first fence on the cross-country.

it is usually developed from an initial lack of understanding of the rider's wishes.

Q. How can I stop my horse from napping?

- You must educate your horse systematically by simplifying your commands. Don't try to tell the horse too many things at once, but instead spell out your requirements clearly.

- For example, once the horse is already napping away from a fence or problem, don't try to out-strength him by pulling him around and riding him back all at once. Instead, out-smart him by first stopping him from running away. Once this has been achieved, turn him. Once this has been achieved then ride him forward and straight in the direction of your choice.

- Always try to put yourself in a position of possible victory so that you can reward achievement, which will build a more willing attitude from your horse.

- Try to think ahead with a horse prone to napping. For instance, don't go deep into a corner near the gate towards home, and find yourself having to make a sharpish turn and losing forward momentum. It would be preferable to make a shallower turn, being smoother and slightly more forward.

- In extreme cases, it can be advantageous to have an experienced assistant on the ground when training. He or she might be able to assist by getting behind the horse and thus help prevent the horse from running away from your requests. They must, however, take great care not to put themselves in harm's way.

- When dealing with a napping horse, don't panic and bustle. Take your time and be prepared to persevere quietly. If a strong reprimand is needed, again be clear and precise. Don't use your whip unintelligently, i.e. as the horse runs away in control of you. As always, try to apply the whip to enforce your leg commands. Be black and white in educating the horse between right and wrong. Don't fudge or cross-apply your aids, and be very quick to reward a positive response from your horse.

- If you are inexperienced and are constantly finding yourself battling with your horse, frequently being frustrated, then seek more experienced help. It may be that a lack of security in your position during this situation is not helping matters.

- Napping can very quickly become a bad habit, learnt as a means of disobedience from an unwilling horse. It can lead to such vices as refusing to leave the security of the yard or the company of other horses when hacking, etc. Once the horse has learned that he can achieve dominance by succeeding to find a way out of working kindly, the problem will need determination and patience to overcome it.

DWELLING OVER JUMPS

Dwelling in the air is when a noticeable decrease in speed or forward rhythm occurs over the fence. Also sometimes referred to as 'hanging up' over the jumps.

Q. What causes the horse to dwell in the air?

• A lack of confidence. This could be as a result of either the fence causing the horse some concern or the rider creating the horse's fear by being weak or not allowing sufficient freedom for a fluent jump.

• A horse that is losing impulsion on the approach to the fence or who is travelling with an insufficient energy level may dwell.

• A horse that is behind the rider's leg may also exhibit dwelling tendencies.

Q. If the horse clears his fences is dwelling a problem?

• Yes, particularly at bigger fences or fences that involve considerable spreads. The dwell could even be more accentuated at unusual fences such as ditches and liverpools.

• Dwelling at individual fences will inevitably escalate to bigger problems when tackling combinations and related distances. The most important stride when riding a related distance is the first stride into the line, if rhythm, balance and regularity of speed are to be maintained.

• A significantly shortened first stride after a dwelling jump will not help in a long-striding combination or at a problem that requires boldness.

Q. How do I prevent my horse from dwelling?

• Look up at the top of the fence or even a bit beyond. Whatever you do, don't look down into the bottom of the jump.

● Think forward. Attempt to slightly increase the impulsion and even the length of the horse's stride on the approach to the jump. Maintain a strong, applied lower leg.

Q. What else can I do to resolve the problem?

● Ensure that the horse is in front of the leg in his flatwork. He must use his own engine and should not require constant reminders to move forward.

● Exercises in upward transitions, extending the stride and sharpening reactions should help.

● It is important that the rider's own position is secure and that the leg is effective. A weak position or loose lower leg over the fence will not assist in maintaining the forward impulsion over it.

● For the more experienced rider the whip could be quietly administered, directly behind the rider's leg at the point of take-off, as an encouragement. The whip is always used right behind the leg, with the hand removed from the rein, as an extension to the leg. This association with the leg will educate the horse to respect the rider's leg in the future.

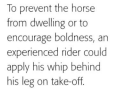

To prevent the horse from dwelling or to encourage boldness, an experienced rider could apply his whip behind his leg on take-off.

- An inexperienced rider must not apply the whip until a totally independent, balanced seat is established and until straightness and control are assured.

- Quiet and consistent repetition over time will help rectify dwelling in a green or suspicious horse.

- If a loss of impulsion or rhythm has occurred over the fence the rider should encourage the horse strongly forward immediately on landing. This will teach the horse that the jump is not the end of the effort or exercise but instead is the midway point.

BUCKING AND REARING

Both of these vices can generally only be exhibited while the horse is not moving positively forward with his hocks engaged.

Except for in extreme instances of fright, most cases of rearing and bucking are antics developed by the horse in avoidance of submission.

Q. What should I do when my horse rears?

- Do not pull on the reins. This may cause him to violently resist your hands and become more energetic in his actions.

- If necessary, grab hold of some mane instead. This will help your own security and balance. Using the reins for personal stability could disrupt your horse's balance and cause him to come over on top of you.

- Wear a neck-strap or breastplate if you anticipate that the problem is likely to occur. You can use these to hold on to when required.

- Ride the horse as positively forward as is practicable. Give him only one set of commands so that he has no reason to be confused. Do not use your hands and legs against each other, pulling and kicking at the same time. Release the hand pressure and apply the leg.

- Be forceful, if required, but never hit your horse about the head. You will be forever regretful if you cause injury to your horse in this most sensitive of areas, particularly his eyes. Only use your whip behind your leg and be quick to reward a favourable response.

- Repeated success by the horse will rapidly manifest into bad habits and must be discouraged immediately. If you are at all frightened or feel unable

This rider is correctly dealing with a rearing horse. She is not pulling on the reins and is trying to ride the horse forward.

to cope with the problem yourself then seek the assistance of someone more experienced. Success of the rider as a result of confident and systematic training will often eradicate the problem quite quickly.

Q. What should I do if my horse bucks?

• Your priority should be to keep his head up. He will buck more easily, and certainly more effectively, with his head down low. Due to your horse's strength advantage you may need to be quite forceful in preventing him from getting his head down.

• Against your likely instincts to want to stop your horse immediately, try to ride him forward. This will enable you to work him through the problem and educate him rather than merely avoid the issue.

• Beware that you do not let playful exuberance lead to serious bucking. This will often occur after jumping while you are slowing the horse down. Ride him forward before executing a correct downwards transition.

2

Rider Problems

LOSING BALANCE

Q. What is the most effective way of remaining in balance?

- To develop an independent balance. Your position should not be dependent on the horse for your security.

- It is essential that your balance is focused on your stirrup, with your weight in the lower leg. Your weight should not be on the horse's mouth or back. Grip at all times with your calves, not your knees. Gripping with your knees will weaken your lower leg contact and prevent your weight from falling into your heel.

- Your lower leg must remain underneath your body weight to give a good base of support.

- There will be little security in the 'seat of your pants'. Sitting in the saddle will cause you to be thrown by the increased effort of the horse's jump or to be left behind the movement.

Q. What should I be doing with my upper body over a fence?

- Very little. Try to remain relatively still. If the approach is made in a light seat with your upper body at approximately a 45° angle to the ground, you need only to fold slightly at the hips.

- Do not throw your shoulders forward at the point of take-off. This could cause the horse to dive or flatten. It could also encourage your lower leg to slide backwards, weakening your base of support and security. You could also run the risk of getting ahead of the movement or even being unseated if the horse refuses.

- Don't lean excessively to one side or the other. This is a habit that is

Both of these photos show horses and riders caught at awkward moments. The rider on the right is in a very precarious position, ahead of the movement, with copious daylight between herself and the saddle. At least she has kept her eyes up and has not inhibited the horse's balance, giving herself a fighting chance.

This horse looks as if he is jumping boldly, which may have caused his rider to fall slightly behind the movement. Her lower leg is ahead of her body weight, not permitting a good base of support for rider independence. She appears to be falling back onto the saddle and using the reins to assist her own balance.

easily nurtured. Try at all times to remain straight in the saddle.

Q. How can I improve my balance?

- Look up. It will help enormously to stay with the movement. Looking down will disorientate you.

• Practise developing independence on the flat by using the two-point position – see also page 40. Work with your stirrups at jumping length and adopt your actual jumping position in trot and canter, standing on the stirrups not sitting in the saddle. If you can't stay independently balanced in trot then you won't over the fence either. It's a simple but revealing test.

• If you fall back into the saddle often, bring your lower leg back. If you topple forward constantly then bring your lower leg forward, relax the knee and drop more weight into your heel for added security.

• Do not rest your weight on your hands or, even worse, on the horse's mouth.

A good cross-country position. The security is focused in the lower leg, with the weight down in the heel. The shoulders are up to prevent being caught ahead of the movement and yet the horse is allowed sufficient freedom. Note that the reins appear to be an extension of the rider's arms.

'DROPPING THE HORSE'

Q. What does 'dropping the horse' mean?

- This is when a rider loses the horse's balance and engagement immediately preceding a fence by dropping his hands completely, thereby abandoning the contact and the necessary rein support.

Q. Why is dropping the horse such a bad thing?

- Eventually this problem could lead to a refusal. As the horse loses his balance prior to take-off, he will inevitably lose his confidence.

- Allowing the horse to fall onto his forehand will never encourage good jumping. The horse must be assisted to maintain his balance and ensure that his weight is over his hindquarters on the approach to the fence to aid his push off the ground by his hind legs when executing a jump.

- Losing the connection between the rider's leg and hand will result in a loss of impulsion.

- Remember, the definition of impulsion is 'contained energy', so abandonment of the hand will disengage the engine and release any power.

Q. What should I do to avoid dropping the horse?

- Try to ensure that a sympathetic contact is maintained on the approach to the fence.

- Remain elastic in your elbows to ensure that the contact is not fixed or restrictive.

- Avoid having loops in your reins.

- Always look up and beyond the fence – don't look down into the base of the fence in your approach.

- Ride forward, keep the horse in front of the leg into a controlling rein contact.

- Improve your own balance. Do not topple forward on approach and drop the reins. Keep your shoulders up.

GETTING LEFT BEHIND

Q. Why do I get left behind when my horse jumps?

• Getting left behind the movement when jumping usually means a lack of independent balance on behalf of the rider. Often it is a result of the rider sitting too far back in the saddle in his approach to the jump with his upper body weight too far behind the leg. This will not give security in the lower leg or a good base of support on which to rely.

• Possibly getting left behind could be the result of approaching a fence too slowly, causing an increase of forward energy while the horse is making his jumping effort. This will cause the rider to be unseated.

Q. What are the knock-on effects of getting left behind?

• Probably the most concerning problem will be catching the horse in the mouth whilst he is making his jump. This will inevitably frighten him sufficiently to cause a refusal as he becomes afraid to take off.

• He may also become frightened by the rider's loss of balance over the jump and react badly on landing, either shooting away from the fence or decelerating noticeably. Obviously this will lead to greater problems when negotiating combinations and related distances. (See Horse Problems – Shooting Away After the Fence, page 19.)

The photo on the left shows the rider unfortunately being caught behind the movement. The next combination shows a more harmonious picture over the same fence.

To develop rider independence of balance, a useful exercise is to ride in the two-point position on the flat (see text).

Q. How can I ensure that I won't get left behind?

- Work on developing an independent balance, particularly on strengthening your base of support in your lower leg and not the 'seat of your pants'.

- Try riding in the two-point position. Ride on the flat with your stirrups at jumping length, abandon any seat contact with the saddle and fully support your weight on the stirrups. Even in trot remain off the saddle (i.e. no sitting or rising). Do not lose the correctness in the horse's way of going because the seat is taken away from you. Maintain his balance and your control.

- If you keep toppling back into the saddle as you do this exercise, bring your lower leg back for more base support. If you keep toppling forward, then your lower leg is already too far back and probably your shoulders are too forward.

- On the approach to the fence, as always, keep your eyes trained up and ahead.

- Try not to get behind the horse's centre of balance on the approach to the jump. Keep the upper body a little forward, approximately at a 45° angle to the ground, to ensure that you will be more ready when the horse jumps.

- Ensure that you approach in a good rhythm with sufficient energy to negotiate the size of the fence easily without a sudden increase of effort being required at the last minute.

SITTING STRAIGHT

Q. How can I ensure that I remain straight in the saddle?

• Always look up and ahead. Looking down will disorientate you and weaken your balance. This is as important throughout the execution of the jump as it is during the approach. Look between the horse's ears.

• Make sure that your stirrups are equal in length and that your weight is evenly distributed between the two.

Probably as a result of applying her whip on take-off, this rider has become slightly crooked. Due to her good training the horse has remained perfectly straight.

- Keep your shoulders in line with your horse's shoulders. For example, as he comes around a corner, your upper body should pivot from the hips to bring your outside shoulder forward of your inside. Do not sit twisted against the direction of movement. When travelling straight your shoulders will be level.

- Do not drop your inside shoulder lower than your outside or collapse your inside hip.

- Do not lean unnecessarily to one side whilst the horse is jumping. Be conscious to fold quietly from the hips, straight forward, without obvious exaggeration.

Q. Will I affect my horse by sitting crooked?

- Almost certainly you will make him crooked as well. He is likely to respond by compensating for your shortcomings, losing his quarters sideways, especially as the rein contact is usually uneven when the rider is sitting crooked.

- Any obvious weight shifting to one side by the rider during the horse's jump will serve to unbalance the horse. He will probably alter direction through the air as a result.

- A rider who sits crooked in the saddle could eventually cause stiffness in the horse, due to his or her own lack of suppleness.

WEAK LANDING

Q. Why do I flop about and become unseated on landing?

- The most probable cause will be that you are not taking the impact of landing on your stirrups but instead are gripping excessively with your knee.

- This can occur when the rider thrusts his shoulders forward when the horse jumps, losing the lower leg backwards. Effectively it would be the same as jumping down from a platform and landing on the ground on your knees.

Q. How can I improve this weakness?

- Work on achieving independent balance. Work in the two-point

position (page 40) on the flat. Strengthen your lower leg by pushing your weight down into your heel and be sure that your lower leg remains underneath your body weight and not behind to offer maximum base support.

• Check that your stirrups are not too long. There must be sufficient angle in your knee to absorb the impact of landing. Likewise, the stirrup should not be too short or your weight may be forced too much into your seat.

• Keep your shoulders still throughout the jump. Slightly up will be better than too low.

Because this rider has not taken the impact of landing on her stirrup, instead pivoting on her knee and losing her lower leg back, she has become weak on landing and in no position to assist her horse into the water.

Riding with stirrups that are too long will not assist with your security and balance. It will weaken your position and make you loose in the saddle.

• Always look up. Looking down will disorientate you and could cause loss of balance on landing.

Q. Could my weakness on landing affect the horse?

• Yes. It could cause him to become frightened by your insecurity. He may begin to rush away from the bad experience, creating control problems, or alternatively he may stop going forward as he is impeded or discouraged by your loss of balance.

• His own balance may be affected in the first few strides after landing, which will not assist rhythmical riding in related distances or in combination fences. Here he will need your assistance.

• The problem could be further magnified when tackling more complicated fences such as drop landings or bounces.

FALLS

Q. How can I avoid a fall?

• Unfortunately you will never be able to completely eliminate the possibility of the occasional unseating. Spills are a fact of life with regard to riding.

• Do not, however, anticipate falling. Always remain positive whenever you ride. Be sensible and avoid unnecessary risks. Develop the most effective position possible through your training, with the focus of your attention on lower-leg security and a good independence of balance. It will help your own balance enormously if you look up, and not down at the ground. Looking down can be disorientating.

Q. Is there anything I can do during a fall?

• Your priority will be to avoid further danger and to minimise the incident where possible.

• Some spills will catch you totally unawares. In these instances you will have very little say in the matter, but at other times, although the fall will seem pretty rapid to an onlooker, it will, in fact, allow you some reaction time.

Falls are inevitable. If possible, put them behind you and focus positively on the next fence.

• Try to land clear of the horse. Do not entangle yourself in his legs by clinging on hopelessly beyond the point of no return.

• Mostly, with a sedate unseating, you **can** be efficient with your body. Tucking up into a tight 'ball', rolling on landing, breaking your fall with body placement, can often be possible to help prevent injury.

Q. What should I do after a fall?

• Check immediately that both you and your horse are unscathed. Be thorough with your investigation, particularly with your horse.

• If unhurt, ideally you should remount, especially in training. In a competition you may not necessarily wish to continue (although completion is satisfying), but it would be a good idea to get back on, canter about or jump a few more fences. This is part of quickly re-building your own and your horse's confidence, and also serves to reduce the significance of the spill itself.

• In extreme cases you may need to reduce the demands by returning to a lower level for further practice, until you feel confident once more.

MENTAL APPROACH

Q. When training, what should I be conscious of with regard to my mental attitude, and how might it affect my horse?

• Your own mental approach will always have a direct influence on the level of success you achieve, both in training and in competition.

• Take responsibility for your actions and endeavour always to convey clarity and consistency in developing communication with your horse.

• Horses do not reason easily so be systematic in your training, and repetitive in your commands to ensure understanding.

• Do not become angry and frustrated if instant success is not achieved. Learn to be patient. Rash decisions and harsh actions may create further problems with trust and harmony.

• Be realistic in your goals to promote enjoyment in your training. Achievement will encourage confidence. Concentrate on your weakness to improve, but do not lose sight of your strengths. Practise these strengths at times during your training sessions. Don't expect perfection at all times or you will inevitably end up disappointed.

• Remain positive in your training. Have conviction in what you are doing. Don't be half-hearted.

Q. How might my mental approach affect my performance in competition?

• As in your training, your attitude in competition will either assist or hinder your level of performance.

• Always try to remain calm, although this is not easy to do in the face of competition. Your tension and anxiety will transmit itself to your horse. With experience, you will be able to find the best methods to suit your own temperament to ensure you remain relaxed. Some will benefit from solitude, others from company.

• Do not be negative in your attitude towards your performance. A positive approach will produce better results. Do not entertain self-doubts. You must believe in both yourself and your horse and have faith in your training and preparation.

Q. What should I do if I suffer a setback?

- Do not dwell on a negative experience. Try to move forward, even turning any mistakes into a positive opportunity. Analyse why the mistake occurred and try to prevent it happening again.

- Readily accept that mistakes will happen, no matter how good you are.

- It may be necessary to consolidate confidence after a setback by reaffirming your skills and understanding at a lower level. You will always know your own enthusiasm for a challenge or readiness to extend yourself if you listen to your own mind.

3

Cross-Country Problems

USEFUL TIPS

- Riding successfully across country requires confidence from both horse and rider as well as a mutual trust. Be prepared to train and practise. Competitions are the testing times, schooling sessions are the educating times.

- Be progressive in your training. Don't miss out any stages of the education. Introduce the horse gradually to any increases in the size and the difficulty of fixed fences.

- Remember, once you have over-faced a horse you may have created a bigger problem that might not be so easily overcome. Don't destroy his trust and confidence by being over-ambitious or reckless. Time spent at the lower levels will be rewarded later.

- Rarely is it possible to dismantle cross-country fences after an unsuccessful attempt in order to lower or reduce the level of the question asked. It may be necessary before tackling fixed obstacles to simulate the likely questions first in the show-jumping arena. For example, use a liverpool (mock ditch) to represent a coffin, construct corners, bounces, wider spreads, etc. that can all be raised or lowered. It will give confidence to both horse and rider to know that they have already developed the necessary techniques for negotiating cross-country obstacles in their flatwork and show-jumping training. The ability to compress the stride, lengthen the stride, increase the impulsion, decrease the impulsion, gain control, go straight, etc. will pay dividends.

- Be prepared to lay a solid early foundation before moving up the levels. There is no substitute for mileage and experience. The education can begin very early by introducing the horse to natural obstacles when out hacking – trotting over small logs, ditches, slopes and banks or walking through water.

Developing a natural feel and instinct is important. This is where hunting the young event horse can be so beneficial.

• When beginning cross-country schooling try to take along a more experienced horse and rider. An anxious horse will gain confidence from a lead given by another horse or will take comfort from the company.

• Eliminate speed from the equation for success. Don't become reliant on speed but instead focus on balance, control, energy and rhythm. This will make for far greater initial safety. Efficiency will lead ultimately to greater speed.

• Some adjustments will need to be made to the rider's regular jumping position when tackling fixed obstacles. Because of the variations of gradients encountered, the likely drops and the banks, and the shift of the horse's centre of balance forward as the stride opens and becomes more galloping, the rider's stirrups will need to be shortened. This will enhance the rider's independence of balance by allowing greater clearance of the saddle with the seat. This in turn will offer increased freedom to the horse. Emphasis will be placed on the rider's lower leg for security and base support with the increased angle in the knee acting as a shock absorber over the undulations, drops, banks, etc.

Before tackling fixed fences, practise at home over show jumps in preparation for the problems you'll be likely to meet on the cross-country. Here the horse is jumping a mock ditch.

- Sitting heavily in the saddle with long stirrups will not assist rider security across country. Instead it will impede the horse's progress.

- As fixed obstacles will not fall down should a small mistake occur, and as the bascule over the fence is likely to flatten a little with the increase of pace, it will be possible for the rider to remain a little more upright with the shoulders to avoid getting caught in front of the movement and unseated.

- It is possibly better to be slightly behind the movement at speed than it is to be ahead of the balance.

- The lower leg can act as a further security base by shifting the heel ever so slightly forward during the horse's jump.

- Gripping with the knee and losing the lower leg back over the fence and on landing will definitely not help. No base will be available to absorb the impact on landing, causing insecurity.

- When cross-country riding always try to be attacking and positive in your attitude, but also think about being in a defensive position. On most occasions everything will go just right, but on the rare occasion that something does go slightly awry, you will be better positioned to remain intact.

DITCHES

Q. When should I start teaching my horse to jump ditches?

- It is never really too early to introduce an inexperienced horse to a small ditch as long as the horse has already completed sufficient education to go straight forward, is respectful of the rider's leg and is able to lengthen his stride when asked.

- First attempt a ditch that is not too deep or wide. A friendly, small, natural ditch would be preferred to a surprising, artificially constructed one.

Q. What techniques do I apply when tackling a ditch?

- Keep your eyes focused on the landing side and do not peer into the bottom of the ditch.

- Looking down will make the problem seem much bigger and more frightening. This will also apply to the horse, who should be encouraged to be

When introducing a young horse to ditches it can be a good idea to offer the horse a more experienced lead. It is amazing how much confidence a horse will gain from seeing another horse jumping successfully in front of him. Eventually he will place as much trust in his rider as he does in the other horse.

brave and forward-thinking, not timid and suspicious. Keep his head up.

• Try to imagine you are simply negotiating a small spread or even just a few rails lying spaced out on the ground. Try to develop a technique where you increase the energy gradually and lengthen the stride up to, over and away from the ditch, just as you would for a wide triple bar. For example, a youngster could start his approach in a controlled trot, nearer the ditch I would encourage a bolder trot (sometimes even a stride or two of canter) and always I would depart from the ditch in a positive canter for some distance.

• Eventually the approach will be entirely in canter with the same principles applied. Begin in an energised but controlled stride, and build into a bigger, more positive canter, lengthening before the ditch, over the ditch and away from the ditch.

• Do not start in gallop, losing speed as you near the hazard before cantering, then trotting, then walking – and even refusing. This would be the opposite of the desired ideal.

Q. What should I do if I suspect that my horse may be nervous or if he refuses?

• Put yourself in a position where you might stand the most chance of success. For example, jump towards home, take a lead from an experienced horse, don't have horses standing behind your approach, but do have a person that can tactfully help and encourage.

• Don't attempt larger ditches until you are sure that a good ditch-jumping technique (as described earlier) has been established.

• Be prepared to spend time and don't be frightened to repeat frequently until ditches become no issue.

• Every success should be rewarded.

• Don't give up easily. Be persistent and try to make each approach by moving slightly forward. It may prove difficult from a standstill. Some momentum will assist the jumping effort.

• If experiencing difficulty don't go too far away to re-approach. Stay near to the obstacle to encourage the horse to face up to the problem. Do not allow him to run away from it.

• The horse may need confirmation of the rider's wishes. If he is unresponsive to the rider's leg, the application of the whip may be necessary. Always use the whip behind your leg and not on the horse's shoulder – it must be clear that the whip is an extension of the leg. For greatest effect apply the whip at the point of take-off; never use the whip after the horse has successfully negotiated the ditch. Once the desired response has been achieved, reward the horse and repeat without the application of the whip.

Q. Do I need to alter my technique for ditches with fences built over them – for example, trakehners and palisades?

• Not really. Still approach on a lengthening stride and don't look down. Focus your eyes and the horse's on the highest point of the jump or beyond. Often the fence itself will assist the ease of clearance by creating more height in the horse's jump.

• Be sure to have the energy level correct – enough impulsion and pace for the effort to be comfortable.

IMPORTANT – DITCHES

- Be positive.
- Don't look down.
- Lengthen the stride in your approach.
- Increase the impulsion.
- Be willing to gain experience and confidence by practising often.

With a solid basic education a horse will ultimately have no fear of ditches, however large.

CORNERS

Q. At what speed should I approach a corner?

- Corners are a test of the rider's and horse's ability to ride with straightness and accuracy. Therefore the pace should be a little restrained to ensure control. A fast, disengaged horse will inevitably lack sufficient accuracy and successful negotiation of the fence will rely largely on chance. Arriving at the take-off spot too far away from the fence could encourage a run-out or a fall, as could arriving too close.

- The stride should therefore remain reasonably collected to ensure an ideal take-off, but should be powerful enough to enable easy clearance of the spread involved.

- Remember that to ride straight you should endeavour to ride forward. Ensure that you are well prepared and in good control well in advance of the jump itself.

Q. How do I choose the correct line?

- It is not possible to approach the front rail of the corner square-on without increasing the risk of landing on the back rail running in the opposite direction. Nor is it wise to approach straight onto the back rail or you will offer the horse the option to run past the fence.

- So, I would dissect the two rails with an imaginary line and would approach perpendicular to this line (see diagram).

- Always familiarise yourself with the correct line and carefully walk the approach before making an attempt, even when schooling. On reaching the

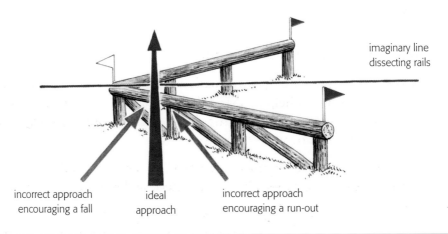

imaginary line
dissecting rails

incorrect approach
encouraging a fall

ideal
approach

incorrect approach
encouraging a run-out

Successful negotiation of a cross-country corner fence.

jump, find your imaginary line, turn your back on the fence and walk directly away from it. Turn around after 10 to 20 metres and look closely at your line. It is not possible to guess the line without looking at the corner angles first.

• To help them find their line more easily, some riders benefit from identifying a fixed object in the distance, beyond the fence about to be jumped. Make sure that this object is fixed (and therefore unlikely to move) and is easily seen well away from the fence. One of the greatest benefits of 'locking on' to the line is that the rider will be looking up, encouraging forward riding.

Q. What can I do to avoid a run-out?

• Apart from ensuring that you approach in a balanced, controlled and yet impulsive stride, it may help to approach on the inside leading leg, i.e. the leg opposite to the point of the corner. This will make running around the fence slightly more difficult for the horse.

• Try carrying your whip in the outside hand. A quiet tap on the shoulder may remind the horse to remain focused ahead and serve to discourage a run-out.

- Always practise exercises for improving straightness (see training exercises) before tackling your first corner.

- This will develop the required technique and boost confidence. Building a corner out of show-jump equipment will enable you to progressively increase the degree of difficulty and size. Start small and narrow until confident before raising and/or widening the exercise.

- Remember to work equally on both left-handed and right-handed corners. Most horses will display a natural tendency to favour one way over the other. Know your horse's weakness.

Q. What should I do if I do have a run-out?

- Apply the recommendations given in the section on horse problems referring to run-outs – that is (in a nutshell), correct the problem by stopping the horse from running away, turn him back towards the fence and indicate clearly that the disobedience has occurred.

- Do not speed up in the second approach if you have experienced a run-out. If the horse has refused but has remained on a straight line (i.e. not run out), your second approach can be more aggressive.

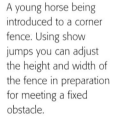

A young horse being introduced to a corner fence. Using show jumps you can adjust the height and width of the fence in preparation for meeting a fixed obstacle.

> **IMPORTANT – CORNERS**
>
> • Ride with controlled, impulsive stride.
>
> • Know your line.
>
> • Ride forward to ride straight.

SPREAD FENCES

Q. What kind of approach should I make?

• Make sure that you are riding with plenty of impulsion (contained energy).

• Ideally try to imagine that you are slightly lengthening your horse's stride up to, over and away from the fence. This does not mean that you should arrive at the fence completely lengthened, but that the horse should be positively in front of the leg and up into the bridle, enabling you to

Spreads need to be approached out of a positive, forward stride to encourage bold jumping.

Whilst spread fences require boldness, they also need engagement of the stride to retain accuracy. A flat or strung-out stride could easily land you in trouble.

lengthen his frame and stride very slightly, without getting any faster. Do not obviously break the rhythm and suddenly accelerate or lose the horse's balance.

- Where the fence is constructed with a sloping profile it is possible to be bolder, riding with enough energy to easily clear the back rail. If the fence has a squarer profile, i.e. incorporating an upright face with width on top, then keep the horse more engaged to ensure accuracy and a more rounded jump.

Q. Do I need to adjust my position?

- Over the top of the jump your position should remain the same as always across country: shoulders up, weight on stirrup with heel down, and lower leg remaining on the girth, not slipping back.

- However, if making a more open approach to a spread fence it is likely that your weight will be initially more forward and off the horse's back, in order to stay with the forward shift of the horse's centre of balance. You will be less inclined to remain in the seat as the stride lengthens.

> **IMPORTANT – SPREADS**
>
> • Ride with impulsion and boldness.
>
> • Have the horse in front of the leg.
>
> • Slightly lengthen the stride without losing rein contact.

UPRIGHT FENCES

Q. What type of approach should I make?

• Because most of the vertical fences we encounter across country are less user-friendly in profile than jumps such as logs, hedges or spreads we must

Treat upright fences with respect. Retain a well-balanced, shortened stride and do not push your horse out of his rhythm. Allow an upright fence to come to you.

treat them with the utmost respect. Try to keep the stride engaged to avoid making a flat jump.

• The horse should be active and must retain his power and balance in his hindquarters. He should not be allowed to fall forward onto his forehand on the approach to an upright.

Q. What speed should I present at?

• Be sure to be unhurried in your approach. Maintain a forward rhythm in a regular, contained stride and allow the fence to come to you. Do not speed up or send the horse on towards the fence, as you would to a spread or a sloping jump.

• Remember that we should only go as quickly across country as safety will allow. It is important to jump cleanly and carefully.

Q. What should I think about with regard to my own position?

• As we collect the length of the horse's canter stride the centre of his balance should move towards his hindquarters. Therefore, it will be necessary to bring your shoulders more upright and your seat closer to the saddle.

• Be sure to keep your lower leg secure and forward in order to absorb any sudden check in momentum should the horse make a mistake and knock the fence with his forelegs.

IMPORTANT – UPRIGHTS

• Keep the canter contained and do not break your rhythm on the approach.

• Be unhurried.

• Remain upright with your shoulders.

BANKS UP

Q. What kind of approach do I need?

- Because it is quite an effort for the horse to jump up a bank, the approach should be made with lots of impulsion. This will give him sufficient energy to easily jump up and land at the higher level, with his undercarriage still underneath his body weight and with the ability to continue forward.

- The face of larger banks can be quite upright in profile so it will be necessary to remain accurate by engaging the canter. Keep the horse's 'spring' half way coiled so as not to let the stride get too long or flat.

Q. What speed should I approach at?

- A good medium pace, controlled enough to keep the connection and accuracy but with plenty of 'oomph' to make the effort comfortable.

Introducing a young horse to a bank. The rider is in balance with his weight well into the stirrup, allowing the horse to jump up freely.

Q. How can I help the horse?

• Always look up. It will help you to ride forward more positively. Don't look down into the bottom of the bank.

• Remain off the horse's back, keeping your weight independently distributed on the stirrups. This will give him the necessary freedom for the effort.

• Ensure that the horse is in front of the leg, not being idle. Strongly apply the leg into a controlling hand to build energy.

• Always ride positively forward immediately on landing up the bank to educate the horse not to lose impulsion. This will be good preparation for banks that have fences constructed on top or for those with several bank steps.

IMPORTANT – BANKS UP

• Plenty of impulsion.

• Medium pace, medium-length stride.

• Light rider position.

• Look up.

BANKS DOWN

Q. What kind of approach should I make?

• Until confidence and trust is established don't approach too fast. Even when experienced the speed will need to be slightly controlled .

• When first introducing a young horse to small banks it will be necessary to negotiate them in trot. This will allow him time to look and assess the problem before he leaps.

• Quietly use the legs to encourage the horse to jump softly out and down the bank.

At the top of this bank, the rider has been caught slightly ahead of the movement. His weight has fallen onto his hands, restricting the horse's freedom, and he has lost the security in his lower leg.

Q. What should I think about in regard to my own position?

• Once you have gauged your approach, try to look forward. Don't peer over the edge and look down. It will only make the drop seem greater and

This rider has fallen forward and is in no position to encourage his horse down the last step. Ideally his shoulders should be back and he should be looking ahead.

will serve to unseat you if the jump is not fluent.

• Take the impact of landing on your stirrups and not on the horse's back.

• It may be necessary to bring your shoulders back a little on the approach and during the actual jump to avoid getting caught ahead of the movement.

• Be prepared to slip the reins quietly through your fingers, if necessary, to give the horse more freedom to stretch his neck down to maintain his own balance. Keeping a tight grip on the reins may pull you forward or inhibit your horse's efforts.

• On landing, close your fingers on the reins, and gather them up to regain control as you ride forward and straight.

IMPORTANT – BANKS DOWN

- Not too much pace.
- Stay back.
- Allow freedom.
- Take the impact of landing on your stirrups.
- Look ahead, not down.

WATER

Q. How should I introduce my horse to water?

- Initial introductions to water should be done quietly and with patience. It is important to build trust and confidence from the beginning.

- It may be necessary to give a green horse a lead from a reliable, experienced horse that can assist in showing a nervous horse that there is nothing to fear. It is remarkable how effectively the green horse gains confidence in seeing that another horse is in no danger or is displaying no concern in what he is being asked to do. On his own, the inexperienced horse cannot be expected to know that the water has a firm bottom and is not too deep.

- Ultimately, as a result of careful mileage, the horse will gain as much trust in his rider as he has in any lead horse.

- As is the case with ditches, it is wisest to attempt a simple natural water hazard such as a ford or shallow river. Don't try and jump immediately in off a bank, but walk quietly into the water instead.

- Once in the water try to walk the horse through or around at a constant pace, instilling a professional, matter-of-fact attitude.

- Be sure beforehand that the water is safe so as not to destroy the horse's trust and confidence from an early bad experience.

- In the initial stages try to introduce the horse to water as frequently as possible. The more often you do it, the less it will be an issue.

Q. How do I begin jumping into water?

- Choose a small, plain bank with a simple approach, preferably at a water complex where an alternative entrance, not involving a jump, is available. Try initially in trot, allowing the horse sufficient time to assess the situation in his approach. Build strength in the final few strides. Don't ride in with too much speed, thereby surprising the horse.

- Be encouraging with your legs and voice to ensure that the horse jumps cleanly in. Repeat until there is no hesitation before attempting the jump in canter.

- When in canter, again don't go too fast. The water could suddenly slow your progress and may cause the horse to lose balance as his legs are held back by the drag effect of the water. Shallow water would be most sensible for an inexperienced horse.

- As the banks become bigger, the principles concerning drop landings will apply. (See Drop Fences, page 80.)

An inexperienced combination tackling a water complex early in their training.

In photo 1 the horse has jumped awkwardly, obviously concerned about the water ahead – a run-out at the next element looks likely. However, photo 2 shows that the rider has not given up trying, and is rewarded by a successful entry into the water (photo 3). Although he has lost his stirrup he is sitting tight and chooses, in photo 4, to direct his horse past the last element.

Q. What should I do if my horse is very cautious about lowering himself into water?

• Ride him more positively forward to encourage him to stretch himself into a jump. It is not sufficient for him to step in, one foot after another.

• Be sure to put him more in front of the leg. It may be necessary to apply the whip quietly behind the leg to demand respect and encourage bravery.

• Once in the water ride the horse forward. Don't let him become too timid or change down too many gears. This will help to prepare for jumping fences sited in water later.

• Look forward yourself; don't look down at the water's edge.

Q. What should I do if my horse launches himself into the water and rushes through?

• This normally happens as a result of concern or fear of the water.

As a general rule in training, once you have presented a horse to a fence, don't give up. However, do not attempt to present to a fence if you are not in a position to help your horse.

A happy combination jumping without concern into water. If you do your homework and gain your horse's trust, water fences should not prove a problem.

• Approach quietly, reducing the speed, and once in the water try to remain there by quietly circling or stopping. Do not let the horse take charge and exit of his own choice.

• Give the horse a pat as a reward and pop out or walk out, then quietly repeat and repeat until the horse becomes more settled.

• Be prepared to slip the reins on entry to ensure that you don't catch the horse in the mouth, and try to land on your stirrups and not on the horse's back.

• There is no substitute for experience.

Q. How do I jump safely out of water?

• Falls out of water are nearly as frequent as falls into water.

• As you travel through the water obstacle try to keep the horse as together as possible, whether in trot or canter – not floundering and disengaged.

• If in canter try to keep the canter short and bouncy.

• Maintain a rhythm and don't anticipate the take-off spot. Your ability to judge distance may be affected by the way the horse reacts to the effects of the water splash, the water depth, etc. Some horses 'back off' the splash and shorten their steps. Others attempt to clear the water and exaggerate their strides. Just maintain balance and connection without losing impulsion and let the bank come up to you.

IMPORTANT – WATER

• Be patient and be prepared to educate.

• Don't ride too fast.

• Keep balance in the water.

• Incorporate drop jump techniques where needed.

FENCES WITH AN UPHILL APPROACH

Q. What kind of approach should I make?

- As a general rule-of-thumb most fences that are constructed on rising ground need to be tackled with plenty of impulsion.

- The natural incline of the approach will probably help to ensure that the horse's weight is better distributed towards his hindquarters, making his driving force more effective. With his forehand lightened you can be bold and kick on.

Q. How will I see a stride to the jump?

- Don't rely too heavily on your eye alone. You may be caught out if the horse's natural stride is shortened by a steep slope.

- Instead be positive and try to ensure that the horse's stride is not too long or flat. Keep the horse's 'spring' halfway coiled. The connection of the horse's stride and frame between your leg and hand will decrease the likelihood of you either standing off or getting too close to your jump. This will also help to build sufficient power for the jumping effort.

Q. How can I assist my horse with my position?

- Be sure not to sit heavily in the saddle. Try to support your own weight on your stirrups but take care that your legs remain active to maintain impulsion.

IMPORTANT – UPHILL FENCES

- Plenty of impulsion.

- Retain engagement.

- Ride light.

FENCES WITH A DOWNHILL APPROACH

Q. How do I keep my horse in balance?

• The biggest problem with downhill fences is the ease with which a horse will fall onto his forehand on the approach, thus leaving his hocks – his essential jumping equipment – trailing behind him.

• Assist the horse to remain balanced on his hindquarters and keep his shoulders light by supporting him lightly with the rein.

• Do not drop the contact and let the horse 'coast' downhill in neutral. Keep him engaged in a low gear.

• Slow down as much as needed to ensure no loss of control or balance. With a green or an awkward youngster it may even be necessary to return to trot if the balance is likely to be lost in canter. This will help horse and rider to gain confidence in one another.

It is very easy for a horse to fall onto his forehand when moving downhill. If the horse is contained between the rider's leg and hand he will have a better chance of keeping his hocks engaged, ready for jumping. This horse risks running into the bottom of the oncoming rails.

Q. How should I introduce downhill fences?

- To start with jump only solid obstacles such as logs, walls, etc. with low heights and friendly profiles. Approach in trot.

- With an inexperienced horse, avoid steep approaches and excessively upright or airy fences. A small sloping palisade would be ideal.

- As the balance and confidence builds you could move from trot to a controlled canter.

- Always go straight on landing to avoid being unseated sideways.

Q. What about my position?

- Be sure to keep your shoulders well up so as not to get ahead of the movement during the jump or to encourage the horse to fall onto his forehand on the approach.

- Try not to sit too heavily on the horse's back to allow him the necessary freedom to bring his hocks underneath him.

- On landing it may be necessary to slip your reins a little to avoid being pulled forward. Don't lose the contact completely or the control will also be lost.

IMPORTANT – DOWNHILL FENCES

- Support the horse.
- Ride with control.
- Slow down.
- Sit up.

COFFINS AND SUNKEN ROADS

Q. At what speed should I come in to the fence?

• It is important that the speed is not too fast. Usually the first element to a coffin combination or sunken road will be quite upright and the ditch or step element unsighted. Therefore let the fence come to you.

• There may be a moment of surprise once the horse notices the ditch or drop beyond the entry rails.

• Too much speed will prevent the horse having sufficient time to assess and evaluate the problems in his approach.

Q. What type of stride should I ride with?

• Try to make the stride as bouncy and energetic as possible while still travelling softly forward.

• Although what lies beyond the initial rails will influence the type of approach made, it should not unduly concern the rider to the extent that a refusal occurs as a result. Be sure then to maintain sufficient impulsion to avoid a stop.

• Keeping the stride short will assist with accuracy in finding a comfortable distance and a clean jump into the combination.

Q. How do I achieve a bouncy canter?

• Be sure to ride the horse's engine, his hindquarters, up underneath him with an active lower leg, into a controlling hand. Do not pull the horse's front end back towards

A successful negotiation of a sunken road complex. (1) The rider is in an excellent position and the entry appears to have been made off a bouncy stride, without too much speed. The horse is already assessing the next problem. (2) The rider's security is in his lower leg and his eyes are looking ahead to the exit and not into the bottom of the road. (3) On landing the rider is being positive but could collect his reins more to 'coil the spring'. (4) The jump up is powerful. (5) As a result of the rider's good lower leg security, his upper body has the flexibility to follow the horse's movement throughout.

his back end. This will be riding 'backwards' on the approach and will be detrimental to maintaining energy.

Q. What about my position?

• It is really important not to get ahead of the movement on the approach to the rails, but it is equally important not to get left behind thereafter. With a secure lower leg it should be possible to be versatile with the upper body to stay with the horse's balance over the 'in' element, the ditch and out.

• As always, look up and ahead to improve your reaction time.

Q. How should I introduce my horse to his first coffin?

• It can be a good idea to practise coffin technique using show jumps on flat ground. Establishing the correct type of stride and pace necessary for a coffin by first attempting fences that can be adjusted in size, will give confidence to both horse and rider later when tackling the real thing.

• As the entry into the combination will most likely be the more difficult section for a green horse, try to eliminate that element from the test. If it is possible to ride past the 'in' question and still present well to the ditch and rail out, then do that first. This will take away the surprise element and establish a confident forward flow through the combination. Once happily jumping the second two elements, the first element can be introduced.

• Thereafter, as is nearly always the case, ride a straight approach to the 'in' rails. Do not angle the first element, otherwise you risk being unseated if the horse touches the fence.

• Before attempting a coffin ensure that the horse is familiar and confident with ditches.

IMPORTANT – COFFINS/SUNKEN ROADS

• Do not approach too fast.

• Create a bouncy and energetic stride.

• Be progressive in your training of coffins/sunken roads.

ARROWHEADS

Q. How might I prevent a run-out occurring?

• Before attempting an arrowhead or narrow-faced obstacle, be sure that you have taught your horse about straightness. When tackling arrowheads you must eliminate crookedness and maximise control so that you are able to influence and guide your horse effectively.

• Develop a good technique to give yourself confidence by frequently practising straight lines in your flatwork and early jump training. Riding pre-specified lines over wide-faced jumps, as described on page 119, will prepare you for tackling an arrowhead.

• If possible to so do safely, I would first approach the narrow panel of an arrowhead in the reverse direction, with the 'arms' of the fence guiding the horse in. Once he is confidently and competently negotiating the fence in a straight manner I would then approach in the conventional direction but with guide poles or wings. These poles can then be placed on the ground to channel the horse straight before being removed altogether.

A narrow arrowhead taken with straightness and confidence in competition.

(1)–(4) Progressive early training for jumping arrowheads. Establish confidence at every step before moving on to the next. (1) First approach the jump with the wings leading you to the arrowhead, i.e. from the wrong direction. (2) Next, approach from the usual direction but with poles guiding you to the centre.

Q. What kind of approach should I make?

- Not too fast, so that you are in control of the situation. Too much speed may cause a run-out.

- The stride should be well connected and not too long, so that accuracy is better assured. A big, flat canter will reduce the likelihood of arriving at the desired (precise) take-off spot.

- Remember that to ride straight it is best to ride quietly forward. Being restrictive or riding backwards in your approach could cause crookedness by losing the quarters sideways. Therefore it is important to establish the stride pattern and speed early on the approach and avoid adjusting or fighting in front of the fence.

- Be careful to sit straight in the saddle and keep a constant, even pressure between both legs and hands to dissuade drifting.

- As always, look ahead and complete by riding straight on landing.

Q. What should I do if a run-out does occur?

- As described in the section on run-outs (page 9) always correct your mistake as it occurs.

- Turn the mistake into constructive training to educate. Don't simply circle around and represent.

- Stop the horse, bring him back on the opposite rein to the run-out and quietly reprimand before trying again. Think about slowing down. Sometimes if the fence is not too big, more success may be achieved in trot

than in canter. It would be preferable that the horse remains straight and stops at the fence than to have the horse take charge and run out. If the horse remains straight and under control, then we can ride more strongly forward at a second attempt.

(3) Then place the guide poles on the ground, still encouraging straightness.
(4) Finally, remove the poles and jump the arrowhead.

• Avoid repetitive, over-schooling of very narrow fences. Eventually your horse may discover the ease with which he can duck out around a narrow obstacle.

• If the horse continues to be inconsistent and unpredictable then more work on straightness with wider fences is needed.

IMPORTANT – ARROWHEADS

- Train for straightness.
- Connect the canter.
- Don't go too fast.
- Prepare and ride forward.

COMBINATIONS INVOLVING TIGHT TURNS

Q. What are the main points to be aware of when tackling turning problems?

• Be sure to gain maximum control before presenting to the fences. Often more haste in executing a series of turning fences will result in less speed. A smooth, efficiently flowing line between fences will maintain regularity of balance and ensure safer jumping than sudden directional changes and abrupt alterations of pace.

• For example, if choosing to execute a time-consuming multi-element alternative, don't hurry but instead be efficient. Just as when driving a car it would be wisest to decelerate into a bend and accelerate out of it. Too much pace at the first element may take you wide through the turn with a lack of control thereafter creating a struggle to present to the next element.

• Always look ahead. Where your eyes are trained is normally where you end up. Be one step ahead of the action with your eyes to speed your preparation and reaction time.

• Try to guide your horse onto an inside leading leg in a turn to aid the forward flow and efficiency. (See Training Exercises – Lead Changes.) Open your inside rein slightly, to indicate early your intention to alter course. Place more weight in your inside stirrup but be careful not to over-compensate and ruin your horse's correct jump.

Q. What exercises might help me to prepare my horse for these questions?

• Any flatwork exercises that encourage suppleness, rideability and control will be useful. You need your horse to accept increased levels of control without resistance. Exercises such as improving the canter (see page 116) and the exercise 'little vertical, big oxer, little vertical' (see page 105) are recommended.

• Ensure that your horse is equally proficient to both sides, left and right. The exercises described on lead changes (pages 107-111) will help.

• Practise bending on circles, ensuring that the horse does not 'fall in' on the inside shoulder. If the horse remains balanced on his inside hind leg, and is bent around his rider's inside leg, he will be more readily able to approach a fence off a turn in a forward manner.

Turning in mid-air. This photo shows too much use of the inside rein. As a result the horse has turned only his head and neck. If the approach to the fence had been slower there would have been more time to guide the horse round with an opening rein. The rider should be looking ahead to the next fence, not down at the horse's head.

IMPORTANT – COMBINATIONS WITH TIGHT TURNS

- Gain control.
- Aim for efficiency not speed.
- Decelerate into turns, accelerate out of them.
- Look ahead.

DROP FENCES

Q. What kind of approach should I make to a drop fence?

- A fence involving a drop landing should hold no perils for a confident horse and a rider who is secure in his position.

- Although the landing at a lower level will influence the type of approach we make, it should not completely override it. There is little point in being over-concerned about the landing if we fail to make a jump in the first place.

- The speed on the approach will need to be slightly reduced to lessen the likelihood of horse and/or rider over-balancing on landing. Remain positive on the approach, however, even lengthening the last strides fractionally to encourage the horse to jump out. This will lessen the steepness of descent and ensure a more secure landing.

Q. How should I adapt my position when jumping a drop fence?

- Just as when jumping down banks it is important not to get in front of the movement. The rider's shoulders will need to remain more upright, folding gently back to compensate for the additional time spent executing the jump onto lower ground. It will become necessary to slip the reins gradually through your fingers to enable the horse to stretch his neck to find his balance on landing. Close your fingers on touchdown to support and regain control.

- Taking the impact of landing on the stirrup is imperative. If the lower leg slides backwards with the main pivotal point of contact being the rider's knee, the increased force of landing may unseat the rider. The stirrup should not be too long; there should be sufficient angle in the rider's knee to absorb the landing without banging heavily on the horse's back.

Q. How often should I practise drop jumping?

- Not too often. Repeating the exercise constantly could ultimately cause physical damage to the horse, especially his forelegs. Moderate practice on good going is acceptable.

- Practising too frequently could eventually make the horse suspicious of the rider's demands if punished often for generously obeying. Keep him happy and confident to respond to your demands.

A young horse jumping confidently off a bank. The rider has allowed freedom without losing the contact and has not got ahead of the movement.

• Try to choose drop fences where the landing is onto ground that continues with a gradual downhill gradient. This will maintain forward momentum better than dropping heavily onto flat ground where the forward flow may be checked abruptly.

• Initially I would choose a drop fence that was solid in construction, such as a log or small ramp as opposed to vertical upright rails. This will encourage the clean, forward technique that is desired.

IMPORTANT – DROP FENCES

• Not too much speed.

• Lengthen stride fractionally in approach.

• Don't get ahead of the movement.

• Allow the horse sufficient freedom.

• Take impact of landing on stirrup.

BOUNCE FENCES

Q. How should I approach a bounce?

• A bounce fence requires an athletic effort from both horse and rider. To achieve this, a good controlled and balanced approach will be necessary.

• Do not ride with too much speed or with a long 'strung-out' stride. Instead try to collect the horse's balance into a 'spring-like' fashion – well contained between your leg and hand while generating plenty of impulsion. This will ensure that you have sufficient energy for the required efforts without the need to resort to speed.

• Remember when collecting the stride and generating impulsion that the ideal is to ride the horse's back end up underneath him into a controlling hand. Try not to ride backwards, pulling excessively and stopping the forward flow.

• Most bounces tend to be upright in construction, therefore the stride pattern should be established early and maintained right up to the point of take-off. Don't break your rhythm on the approach by suddenly sending your horse on, or alternatively by decelerating at the last minute. Sending him on will flatten his stride and decelerating will lose your impulsion.

• If the bounce involves spread fences or if the distance between the two elements is generous then you can afford to ride a little more boldly.

Throughout this bounce sequence the rider has remained well in balance with a good position. However, it appears that the horse is reaching for the second element, indicating a slight lack of impulsion.

Q. What about my own position?

• Independence of balance is very important. Your weight should remain focused on your stirrup throughout, with your upper body remaining over the centre of the horse's balance. Try not to get left behind and impede your horse's progress, and conversely don't anticipate and get ahead of the movement.

• Because it will be necessary to make the approach on a contained stride with the balance on the horse's hindquarters, the rider can bring back his upper body.

Q. How can I further help my horse successfully negotiate a bounce?

• Be sure to maintain a strong, encouraging lower leg from start to finish. Don't remove your leg as he jumps the first element. This will allow the forward impulsion to dwindle. Your horse will require direction to jump the second element also.

• Do not abandon the horse with your reins (see 'Dropping the Horse', page 38). If the horse is to remain 'spring-like' then he will require some support from the hand to stay collected between the jumping efforts. Be sure, though, not to inhibit the horse by being over-firm with the rein contact.

Q. How should I begin teaching my horse to bounce?

• I would begin either in the show-jumping arena or with some low, natural logs in the open. With show jumps the heights and distances can be varied and, obviously, a mistake will be of less consequence.

• A small bounce incorporated into a gymnastic exercise where you will arrive on an assured rhythm and correct stride may help give both horse and rider confidence by allowing some natural flow.

• Allow the first element of the bounce to be somewhat lower than the second element. This will encourage the horse to enter the exercise more freely. If his eye is drawn significantly towards the second element he will be less likely to hit a lower element and should be able to be ridden a fraction more strongly throughout.

• Remember to ride positively away from the exercise to ensure no loss of rhythm or energy, especially if a small mistake has occurred.

Q. What should I do if I stop at the first element?

- Check that you are not dropping your horse or allowing the 'spring' to uncoil on the approach.

- Try to build up more impulsion and engagement by kicking the horse more into the rein.

- Keep your eyes up and be more positive. It may be necessary to lower the obstacle initially until forward momentum is restored.

Q. What should I do if I stop at the second element?

- Be more aggressive. The hard part (i.e. the first element) is behind you. Don't look down, apply your leg immediately on landing over the first element – you may even need a little assistance from your whip.

- Avoid more speed. This may cause you to over-jump the first element, which in turn could cause further difficulties by placing you too close to the face of the second element.

IMPORTANT – BOUNCE FENCES

- Not too much pace but plenty of impulsion.
- Retain a 'spring-like' stride.
- Sit up and remain independently balanced.
- Do not approach crooked.

FENCES WITH A ROOF ABOVE

Q. How will my horse react to a jump with a roof above it?

- Without actually practising over one you won't really know. There is nothing more complicated than usual in the actual jump, however, the strangeness of the surroundings and the effect of a confinement of space may cause the horse concern. As is always the case with unusual fences, a

A nice training fence with a high, airy roof above, ideal for introducing a young horse to roof fences. Here it would be possible to first walk the horse under the roof and around the fence before jumping.

sympathetic introduction to the problem and then further gradual education will develop the horse's trust in his rider and his confidence to obey.

• Some horses never show any concern whatsoever. Others are never totally comfortable with the confinement of space throughout their whole eventing career.

Q. What should I be aware of when approaching the jump?

• Be wary that the horse may make a crouching jump. Because of the roof above he may show a reluctance to jump high up into the air.

• Approach without too much speed. This will allow him sufficient time to assess and comprehend the unusual circumstances. Also there will be the possibility of changing light or shadows. Speed will cause confusion and concern.

Q. How should I introduce my horse to this type of fence?

• Very few of us are fortunate enough to have our own cross-country training facilities, but don't leave experimentation until you go to a competition, when you will be forced to approach only once under pressurised conditions.

With good training the horse can become confident enough to tackle owl-holes such as this.

• Try to locate a small, easy fence with a roof well above it where you can freely run though your education programme. For example, if the construction allows, start by walking under the roof first, beside the fence. Progress to trotting over the fence, possibly even with the lead of an experienced horse, before finally cantering over it.

• If the homework is done initially and a solid foundation is laid it is probable that you will never encounter problems later. Nowadays some of the questions asked – for example at key-hole or owl-hole type obstacles – appear unnaturally tight.

IMPORTANT – FENCES WITH A ROOF

- Approach without speed.

- Let the horse assess the fence and familiarise himself with the confinement.

- Don't wait to try out your first roof fence at a competition. Spend time practising under roofs in training.

STEEPLECHASE

Q. What should I be aware of when steeplechasing?

- Do not become reckless.

- It is important not to be consumed by the need for increased speed at the expense of the fundamental elements for safe cross-country riding.

- Do not abandon the basic requirements of rhythm, balance and **control.**

- Steeplechasing should be seen merely as an extension to bold riding. Mostly the fences will be sloping in profile and constructed from soft brush materials, so the principles for riding spread fences (see page 57) should be adhered to. The stride on the approach should be subtly lengthened to ensure scope enough to maintain flow across the obstacle within the pace and rhythm. This can only be achieved if the gallop is not strung-out or if the rider has control. The stride must never become totally flat and disengaged.

- Lack of control will invite inaccuracy.

- Ideally, the rider should kick on and lengthen whenever he is unable to judge a suitable distance to take off on for the fence. However, if the stride pattern is already strung out, he will be taking a risk. Risks should be avoided. Safety is paramount. Therefore be prepared to gently decrease your speed in an emergency. If this is achieved without causing resistance or without dramatically altering the horse's rhythm, the probability will be a successful, fiddled jump. Thereafter the gallop should be corrected to ensure

A steeplechase fence being taken with confidence and boldness.

a more effective stride. Better engagement, more control and an established rhythm will enable you to lengthen to your fences again.

- The rider's stirrups should be slightly shorter than cross-country length. This will ensure that the rider can remain over the horse's centre of balance as he moves forward with the opened stride of gallop.

- Be willing to practise steeplechase technique. A single fence is sufficient for beginners.

IMPORTANT – STEEPLECHASE

- Do not lose the basic elements of control, balance and rhythm.

- Try to lengthen your stride on the approach.

4

Problems Arising at Competitions

EXCESSIVE TIME FAULTS

• This should not be considered a major problem during the early stages of training or introduction to competitions.

• First, a good balance should be established, control gained and rhythm achieved. From that point speed can be easily increased without jeopardising performance or safety.

• Losing control, balance and rhythm will actually slow you down. Fighting against the horse to gain dominance will not allow forward riding.

• Do not ride in a stop-start manner. Maintain a flowing rhythm. Sprinting between fences then wrestling for control in front of the jumps will ultimately slow you down.

• The further back from the fence that you need to begin setting up the balance and control, the slower you will go. It is better not to lose the necessary ingredients for good jumping during your gallop between the fences.

• Only when you are confident that you are in control and in a good balance but are still not achieving times near to the optimum should you consider methods of improving your time.

• First check that you are taking the most direct routes feasible between the fences. Take care not to go unnecessarily wide on bends where no jumping efforts are required. Don't meander about. Keeping your eyes up, looking ahead, will help.

• When walking the course, occasionally look back to the previous fence. Judge if you have arrived at that point via the most direct route. You may save valuable seconds without going any faster.

- When you become competitive and increase your speed, do so initially after the jumps and not towards the jumps. Take the time you need to negotiate the fences cleanly and correctly.

- By not wasting time after the jump you could save a second per fence – nearly half a minute over the entire course. Press on deliberately on landing so you are in full stride immediately. This will also remind you to remain forward-thinking between the fences without letting the tempo slacken.

- Don't waste valuable seconds on landing languishing over the glory of successful negotiation. Reward yourself and your horse as you move positively on. Taking four or five strides to get going again will waste time.

- At home familiarise yourself with the speed required for your level. Mark out a specific distance from A to B, say 490 metres = pre novice, or 570 metres = intermediate. Then, with the use of a stopwatch, ride at the pace you think you should be travelling. It should take you one minute from point A to point B. Practice will give you a more natural feel and understanding.

- Remember there will be slow areas on the course, twisting through woods, sharp bends or steep gradients. It will not always be possible to travel at the optimum speed. Take care not to be travelling too fast for the terrain or conditions, but, without breaking your rhythm excessively, try to utilise the open, flat and straight sections.

TENSION

- It is inevitable that young or inexperienced horses will become affected by the atmosphere surrounding competition conditions. Large groups of horses, loudspeakers, applause, etc. can initially seem foreign and daunting.

- It is near impossible to re-create this atmosphere at home in your preparation, so be willing to undertake this part of the horse's training and education away from home or during competition.

- Always try to remain calm yourself. Any obvious rider tension or attitude changes will transmit themselves to the horse, confusing him.

- Arrive at the competition in plenty of time so as to avoid the pressure of time restrictions. Rushing will cause panic reactions in both horse and rider.

- Don't expect immediate attention or submission. It is natural for an intelligent horse to show some interest in his surroundings. Perhaps ride him about on a loose rein, allowing him to become familiar and comfortable with the additional distractions. Then he will be more likely to maintain concentration once you begin schooling or working in.

• If tension is expected from the horse through earlier temperament indications, it may be a good idea to lunge him before riding. This will reduce the likelihood of confrontation between horse and rider at a time when nerves may influence either one's thinking. Lungeing may serve both to settle the horse, by taking the edge off energy-wise, and to promote relaxation, mentally and physically.

• Try to ride the horse as 'normally' as is practicable. Don't abandon the basis of your training.

• Accept that the horse will possibly become more self-motivated and forward-thinking. Although you will be riding with much subtlety and encouraging relaxation, don't stop riding forward and maintain a steady lower leg. Acceptance of the rider's leg should still be a consideration if you want to avoid over-reaction to an applied aid.

• Quietly occupy the horse's mind, being gradual in the difficulty of your demands. Circling, lateral work, transitions, etc., will require attention and response while still promoting forward riding with control.

STARTING-BOX DILEMMAS

• The problem of not being able to get into the start box, or losing control of the horse once inside it, is a situation that can occur very quickly. Often the problem is created unwittingly by the rider himself. As always, a good steady education will pay dividends.

• Over-eagerness on behalf of either the horse or the rider must be tempered. Rearing and napping are displays of inability to cope with the pressures of the impending excitement. The rider can contribute hugely to this through his own intensified emotions.

• The pressure must be reduced.

• Arrive at the start box in plenty of time. Arriving late and in a hurry will contribute towards the horse sensing tension and urgency. He will learn quickly what to expect if he is rushed in and then out again even faster.

The horse on the left is showing tension in the start box, whereas the horse on the right looks calm and unconcerned. Take time in your horse's early education to make sure that going into the start box does not become an issue.

• Walk quietly near the entrance to the box a few times before entering. Perhaps walk a few circles nearby and trot some quiet lines away from the box and towards the box.

• Ask someone experienced to lead the horse in if he is likely to be nervous about the confined space or excitable. Your helper could even stay with you to calm and comfort the horse.

• Stand facing the back of the box in a relaxed manner. When turning to exit, try to walk a circle rather than spin the horse around, and if the horse anticipates the start, don't allow him to blast out. That will make the next time all the more difficult.

• In extreme cases, you may need to leave the box in trot, gradually gathering momentum. Horses do learn from repetitive training, both good and bad.

• In most instances, a horse displaying uncontrollable behaviour during the start at a competition would probably exhibit no such problems if taken back there the next day, without the distractions surrounding the competition atmosphere. This would indicate that the problem is about the associated issues rather than the start box itself.

SPOOKINESS

- Avoid direct confrontation with the horse and the object of his concern. Aggressively riding straight at spooky objects will probably only compound the matter short-term and create further problems in the future.

- Try to remove the focus of attention away from the horse's phobia and get his concentration back on you instead. If, for example, he is shying at a banner or sign on the outskirts of the course, bend him away from the problem around your leg. Focus his attention in the opposite direction to the object and ride him forward past the problem.

- Do not speed up, especially if your horse is likely to spook during his presentation to a particular fence. Allow him sufficient time to assess the problems and deal with his concerns while he moves steadily forward. Rushing him may invoke a negative response.

- Give your horse enough mileage to develop his trust and confidence in you, his rider. For example, in your training it may be necessary to introduce him to spooky objects whilst schooling. Perhaps ride a circle near an unusual object that will gradually bring him closer to the object without obvious confrontation. Maintain his concentration throughout and be prepared to repeat a presentation frequently. Try not to pressurise the horse. Take your time and be patient.

LOSING CONTROL

- Many horses, when affected by the exciting atmosphere of competition will become much stronger than they are normally in their home environment.

- Often the rider's own competitive nature or his/her increased anxiety can be a contributing cause to this problem.

- Do not completely blow your horse's mental stability or abandon your good training in the heat of the moment. If you do discover that your are losing control, you may need to curb both your own and your horse's enthusiasm and re-establish your balance and rhythm. There will be time later to introduce speed once control is gained.

- Try not to raise your hands high and match your horse in a battle for strength. He will inevitably win out.

• Keep your hands low into the horse's neck. Slight jockeys are able to 'hold' highly trained, pulling racehorses by using bridged reins. A full bridge is impractical for cross-country with its many turns, banks, drops, etc. However, a half bridge can be quite useful. With a short rein, place one fist into the base of the horse's neck just in front of the withers. Now he will be pulling against his own weight, allowing you to conserve your strength.

• A stronger bit may be required as safety is of paramount importance, but do not assume that this will always be the only answer. If the problem lies in the horse's head you may eventually spoil his good mouth by over-bitting him. Seek an experienced opinion on bitting matters, and do not be hasty to give up on your training.

TIPS ON WARMING UP

• Allow yourself sufficient time to complete your preparation. It would be better to slow your warm-up down with some relaxed periods of walking than to be rushed and anxious.

• Be progressive in your warm-up.

• Start slowly with some basic flatwork to loosen up your horse before you begin any jumping. Towards the end of your warm-up, move the horse up a gear or two to open him up towards gallop. This will prepare him both physically and mentally for the cross-country start.

• Jump the practice fence initially out of a comfortable rhythm, at a moderate pace and stride. A couple of times will establish your confidence. Then use the same fence to 'tune' you both for the problems ahead. Try to execute a bolder jump by lengthening your stride on the approach. Try to contain the stride and maximise control, perhaps by making a closer turn into the practice fence.

• Ride a diagonal line over the fence to confirm straightness.

• Repeat any warm-up exercise you are not happy with until satisfied, so that you set out on the course in a positive frame of mind.

• In the warm-up area at competitions, be very aware of other riders also engaged in their preparations. Do not ride others off their lines or walk across the face of the fences without paying due care and attention.

TIPS ON WEATHER AND GROUND CONDITIONS

• When weather and ground conditions are less than ideal, you will need to make some subtle minor adjustments, but do not attempt to completely alter your established way of going. Slight modifications based on the problems presented will be sufficient.

• When raining heavily, when the footing is loose or when the ground is slippery, slow down a little. This will increase control, encourage stability and reduce risks.

• In wet conditions do not abandon your horse by riding with loose reins. Instead keep him well supported between your leg and hand.

• Maintain a stride that is a little more collected than considered normal to prevent excessive slipping and sliding.

• Ensure that your rein contact will not be affected by the wet. Rubber-gripped reins are advisable; smooth-palmed leather gloves are not.

• When the ground is excessively muddy or the going is deep and holding, do not lose impulsion. Endeavour to increase the energy levels to compensate for the additional effort required to execute the jumps. Try to 'coil the spring' and engage the horse's hocks to produce more power without resorting to more speed.

• Be positive and try to maintain forwardness. Don't decelerate suddenly in front of your fences, as doing so will allow the impulsion to decrease.

• In very hot and humid conditions, be aware that your horse may tire more easily. Throughout your performance maintain an easy rhythm that can always be increased towards the end of the course, if necessary.

• You may wish to curtail your warm-up in hot conditions to conserve more energy for the competition itself.

• Anticipate increased sweating when hot and humid. Take the same precautions with regard to the grip on the reins as you would in the wet. Sweaty reins will also prove slippery and although your may prefer less clothing, gloves will remain essential.

• Make ample provision in the hot for cooling your horse down after his performance. Use plentiful water, and ice if available, to return your horse's temperature level to normal. Keep him gently moving while his respiration also stabilises.

• Be conscious of the effect that very firm going will have on your horse's performance. Do not punish him by jumping him unnecessarily or jarring may result. Ride with discretion and do not ride frequently with speed, especially when negotiating drops and banks.

• Choose studs applicable to the ground conditions. Use squarer wedges and larger sizes in heavy going, and use sharper, more pointed ones for slick and slippery footing when ground penetration is required for security.

TIPS ON WALKING THE COURSE

• If you are inexperienced, try to walk the course with someone more knowledgeable than yourself. He or she will be better equipped to detect problems that you may not recognise, and may be able to offer advice on finding solutions.

• Pay particular attention to your initial impression of a fence, and your immediate reaction to the first sighting. Remember, your horse will not have the opportunity to walk the course so in competition he will be seeing the fences for the first time. When walking, try to see the jumps through your horse's eyes as well as your own.

• Don't meander around the course in large groups or even socialise. Focus on the task in hand, walk promptly and concentrate.

• Walking briskly will give you a better overall concept of the total course layout. Avoid frequent interludes or a leisurely approach.

• Pay attention to the route, the ground conditions and any hazards between the fences, as well to the jumps themselves.

• Take note of the numbering of all of the fences as you proceed round the course so that you do not miss out any obstacles.

• Choose any line or option that will best suit you and your horse's strengths and weaknesses. You will probably be the best judge of these, so don't be unduly persuaded against your judgment by outsiders. Listen to respected advice but don't be concerned with countless suggestions from uninformed sources.

• Don't dwell at any particular fence. Take sufficient time to assess all possibilities and to analyse problems, but reach a decision and move on. Standing gazing into a deep ditch or spending unnecessary extra time will only de-focus you from the real issues.

• If you walk the course the day before you compete, be aware that ground and weather conditions may change overnight. Be aware of possible light changes between sunny and cloudy weather and note the sun placement above obstacles at the time of day you will be competing.

• Occasionally look back in the direction you have come from as you approach a fence. This will help you tighten up your line between the jumps by ensuring that you have walked the most efficient or suitable route. It is easy to wander off course, especially if you look down whilst walking.

• Notice where on the course you may encounter slow or fast sections. Twisty areas, such as through trees, will require care. So try to highlight any open or galloping areas where you might compensate by speeding up.

• Be aware of where the course requires more or less energy from your horse. Is there a long, uphill stretch? Is it towards the beginning of the course, or at the end? Use your common sense to devise a suitable game plan.

• While walking your course visualise your impending performance. Be positive about it.

• Once your course walk is completed, take time to digest all that you have seen. Run through the entire course in your head as though you are riding it. This should take you nearly as long to execute as it will when actually riding.

TIPS TO AVOID ELIMINATION

• Read your affiliation rule book. Know all the rules pertaining to acceptable tack, behaviour, horse and rider qualifications, etc. If you are in any doubt, ask the event's technical delegate.

• Walk your course thoroughly. Do not miss out any obstacles, any part of an obstacle, or compulsory flags. Do not jump a fence in the wrong direction direction or out of numbered sequence.

• When walking the course, do not alter anything relating to the obstacles. Removing hazards, shifting shrubs or branches, etc. may give you a better line or meet with your own approval, but these hazards may, in fact, be part of the course designer's intended questions. Any issues regarding safety, such as holes, sharp objects, etc. should be referred to the technical delegate.

• Familiarise yourself with the numbering of the obstacles, especially at combinations. Be aware of the flagging for each jumping effort. You must pass between every set of flags on the entire course, leaving all white flags to your left and all red flags to your right.

• If the event is staging more than one grade of competition, be sure you know which coloured numbers and which flags relate to your class.

• Check all the alternative routes, both at the multi-complexes and at the single fences. If you are unsuccessful with your first choice of line you may fair better tackling a different option.

• Remember that when jumping combinations it is not necessary ever to retake part of an obstacle already negotiated (unlike in the show-jumping arena). In some instances, however, such as with bounces and steps, it may be preferable to start again from the first element. This is indeed allowed. Most often, though, it is easier simply to attempt the remaining un-jumped elements.

• Retaking a single fence already jumped results in elimination.

• If you are unlucky enough to part company with the horse, be aware of which side of the fence your horse has ended up – the take-off or the landing? You must pass through the flags together!

• Avoid turning circles once presented to an obstacle or whilst tackling combinations. Although only penalised as a refusal, a circle could ultimately contribute to an elimination as a result of three refusals at one fence or an accumulative five refusals in total on the course.

• Be at the start on time.

• Outside assistance is forbidden whilst you are mounted, except for the returning of spectacles, whips and safety headgear. While dismounted, help is allowed in catching your horse, adjusting tack or in getting remounted. Remember that outside assistance can include any verbal instruction or directions.

• You will be eliminated from the competition for riding dangerously or for excessively pressing a tired horse. In the interests of both your horse and yourself, readily accept that there will be future opportunities and retire.

Training Exercises

TRAINING TIPS

- Always be progressive in your training. Do not leave gaps in your education by missing out stages in your development or by being over-ambitious.

- Training is the time to supply information and to establish understanding. Competitions are the tests of the level of training achieved.

- Throughout your training, endeavour to produce a generally correct way of going, i.e. promote balance, rhythm, control, athleticism, etc., but try also to be specific to your own horse's individual needs.

- Be systematic in your approach and analytical of results. Plan your training exercises in advance and digest the outcome.

- Be sympathetic and show patience. Some issues will take longer to resolve than others. Remember, riding is meant to difficult, otherwise everybody would do it!

Treat each horse as an individual and vary your training accordingly. A horse who rushes his fences or who is strong will require different training to one who is cautious or lazy.

TRAINING EXERCISE 1

DOUBLE BOUNCE FROM TROT

Equipment
6 jump wings
5 poles

Exercise construction

Single rails are placed on cups between the wings at a consistent distance to make two equal bounce efforts (see diagram). Normally an effective distance would be approximately 11 feet (3.3m), but this could be adjusted fractionally, according to the type and size of horse. No ground rails are needed underneath the raised rails, but a ground pole is placed at 9 feet (2.7m) on the approach with another on the landing side of the bounces.

I would rarely raise the bounces above 2 feet 6 inches (75cm) high. More often than not 18 inches to 2 feet (45–60cm) would be sufficient.

Exercise benefits

• To improve the horse's sharpness of technique.

• To improve the horse's athleticism.

• To establish a rhythm and constant pace.

• To encourage elasticity in both horse and rider.

• To ensure the rider's independence of balance.

Points of awareness

• The approach should be in a controlled rising trot.

• A soft aid to canter should be applied over the initial trot pole.

• The horse should finish the exercise by landing inside the final ground pole and leave the fences in an engaged canter.

• The horse should not drop behind the rider's leg and fall into trot following completion of the exercise.

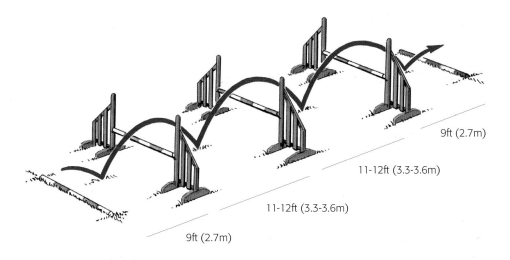

9ft (2.7m)

11-12ft (3.3-3.6m)

11-12ft (3.3-3.6m)

9ft (2.7m)

- The horse should stay straight throughout and in the centre of the fences.

- The rider must maintain independent balance on the stirrup and remain over the centre of the horse's balance.

- Avoid pushing the shoulders forward, losing the lower leg backwards, having a heavy seat contact with the saddle, and lengthening reins.

- Consistent hand contact with elastic elbows will regulate pace, and lower leg pressure will ensure that impulsion is maintained as required.

- The connection between the rider's leg, the horse's hind legs and the rider's hands should be softly enhanced.

The double bounce from trot exercise being successfully negotiated by a young horse.

TRAINING EXERCISE 2

VEE POLES

Equipment
2 jump wings
5 poles

Exercise construction
A normal vertical fence can be erected, preferably with a ground line. A symmetrical vee is then constructed by resting two additional poles on the top rail of the vertical, protruding forwards from the centre of the face of the fence and widening out at ground level (see diagram). The narrowness of the vee, both at the point of contact with the fence and at the ground level, will be in direct relation to the severity of the horse's problems.

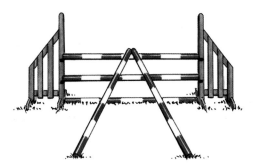

Exercise benefits

- To slow down the approach of an over-enthusiastic or rushing horse.

- To improve the technique, particularly the front legs, of a careless horse.

- To correct crookedness or drifting.

- To encourage a slower more deliberate jump.

Points of awareness

- This exercise would not be used with a timid, 'backed off' or nervous horse.

- The vee pole should create a more claustrophobic area of take-off for the horse, causing him to slow down, place more weight on his hindquarters

This horse is showing increased lift with his forearm and a nice bascule, assisted by the vee poles. The vee pole exercise is most effective for horses that rush or are careless with their technique.

before jumping, gain more height during the first half of his bascule and gain increased focus of attention on the fence.

- The vee poles will duplicate the effect of the rider's hands; less restraint should be necessary, creating a softer approach and jump.

- Straightness is encouraged because the poles prohibit drifting left or right.

- Vee poles can be utilised on single fences as well as in lines, and also with oxers occasionally, being careful not to frighten the horse.

TRAINING EXERCISE 3

DIAGONAL POLE ON OXER

Equipment
4 jump wings
5 poles

Exercise construction
Build a regular square oxer at the desired height, with a normal ground pole placed at the base of the approach side, then lay a further rail diagonally on top of the oxer, from one front corner to the opposite back corner.

The use of a pole laid diagonally across the top of an oxer will improve the horse's technique. The horse will be required to show more respect for the front rail, encouraging him to back off very slightly.

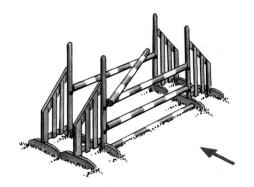

Exercise benefits

- To improve the horse's jumping technique and bascule.

- To encourage the horse to have more respect for the front top rail.

Points of awareness

- The diagonal pole should encourage the highest point of the horse's bascule to be shifted towards the front of the oxer instead of to the middle or back.

- The weight of the additional rail on top should secure the front rail, making it less likely to be knocked down. This will create more respect in the horse, usually noticeable on the horse's second attempt. This will be equally effective for lazy front or hind legs.

- The rider should make his approach in a forward canter and try to arrive at a deep take-off spot. Standing the horse off from the base of the fence will not encourage the horse to fold his forelegs quickly or tidily.

- The horse should remain straight over the fence.

- The diagonal pole should encourage additional height to the horse's jump.

- To jump the fence in both directions, place a ground pole on each side (see photo above).

TRAINING EXERCISE 4

LITTLE VERTICAL – BIG OXER – LITTLE VERTICAL

Equipment
8 wings
2 planks
6 rails

Exercise construction

First build an oxer from the two planks. It is more effective not to use a ground rail.

The oxer can be built at whatever height is desired by the rider, although for the first few attempts it should not be too large. Once confident jumping is established over the oxer, construct a small vertical fence at a distance of 42 feet (13m) each side of the oxer, at approximately 2 feet (60cm) high. The distance of 42 feet (13m) is deliberately short for three strides.

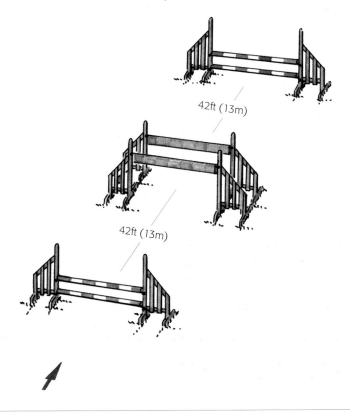

42ft (13m)

42ft (13m)

Exercise benefits

- To improve the elasticity of the horse's canter.

- To encourage more controlled impulsion within the canter.

- To improve the horse's jumping technique.

- To ensure the rider's independence of balance.

Points of awareness

- The approach to the first small vertical should be made in a contained, controlled canter. After the horse pops the first vertical, the canter should be maintained to the oxer and then also maintained from the oxer to the last vertical.

- The rider must use sufficient leg to maintain enough energy to clear the oxer easily.

- Immediately on landing from the oxer the rider must re-engage the horse's hindquarters and condense the canter before the vertical.

- Ideally if the rider has been effective in the first stride after the first vertical, the second and third stride preceding the oxer can be ridden with a softening hand and a closing leg to encourage the horse to make a powerful, yet soft jump.

- When condensing the stride between the vertical, the oxer and the vertical the horse should always remain straight. The rider should not create undue resistance. The horse should stay round and soft in his frame and stride.

- The rider should remain independently balanced with the focus of his balance being placed on the lower leg. By riding with a light seat, the horse will receive the freedom to make a good bascule over the oxer.

- When the exercise is completed the horse and rider should continue in a straight line, further engaging the canter to make a transition back to the walk or a halt on the straight line, not using a corner. As the horse comes back and engages before the transition he should come light in the rein. He should not drop behind the leg and fall into trot.

- The rider must keep his eyes up over the oxer to avoid being unseated.

- If the horse becomes anxious or unsure of his jump, a ground rail could be used at the oxer to help him regain confidence. Alternatively the oxer could be lowered and/or the distance between the fences made more generous.

TRAINING EXERCISE 5

LEAD CHANGES (1)

Equipment
2 jump stands
3 rails

Exercise construction
Build a simple vertical fence with a generous ground rail. The fence should be at an easy height for the level of experience.

Exercise benefits

- To increase lateral suppleness.

- To ensure equality of balance.

- To improve rideability.

- To promote forward preparation.

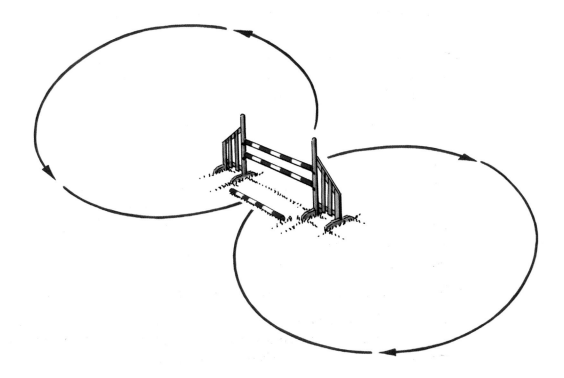

Points of awareness

- Riding a figure of eight that incorporates the fence at the cross-over point, approach perpendicular to the face of the jump.

- Think ahead to the change of direction on landing, left to right or right to left.

- Flow evenly around the circle at a controlled pace allowing plenty of time and space. Maintain a constant rhythm throughout.

- Prepare for the change of direction by first looking purposefully in the direction you wish to go.

- Almost exaggerate this to open up an early feel for the new desired direction. Using a slightly opening inside rein, quietly guide the horse into the intended turn. Do not disturb the bascule by pulling excessively on the rein. Place increased weight into the new inside stirrup to indicate to the horse your intended new direction.

- Do not exaggerate a lean to the side with your upper body. This could have an adverse effect of unbalancing your horse.

- Once you have achieved the change of leading leg on landing, continue straight ahead before turning with a good bend around your inside leg.

- If you do not achieve the desired new lead then ride straight ahead before circling round to try again.

- In cases of extreme stiffness it may be helpful to lay a diagonal ground rail underneath the fence to lead the horse towards the new direction. If the approach was made off the left lead, for example, the ground pole should lie with the right end in front of the fence and the left end behind it.

- It is equally important that the horse can still jump softly from one leading leg and land on the same leading leg at the rider's request (i.e. not changing leads or direction).

- When not changing direction, but when jumping on a circle, do not allow the horse to jump out through the outside shoulder, away from the leading leg, in a stiff manner.

- Be sure to maintain a gently guiding, open inside rein, with your weight more into the inside stirrup and your eyes looking in the desired direction.

- Regardless of the direction after the fence when approaching off a turn, bring the horse through the turns with both reins. Do not simply pull with the inside hand, but instead also guide the horse around with the outside rein against his neck to prevent him losing his balance through the shoulder.

- Keep the outside lower leg slightly behind the girth to prevent the quarters swinging out.

- Be sure to work equally in both directions.

This photo shows the rider changing lead from the left leg to the right. The new inside rein could be a little more open to indicate the change of lead. Note that the fence has two ground rails, enabling it to be jumped from both directions.

TRAINING EXERCISE 6

LEAD CHANGES (2)

Equipment
10 jump wings
8 poles

Exercise construction
First build a cross-pole on the centre line of a wide arena or field. Three or four strides from the cross-pole, on an arc, build an oxer both to the left and to the right. Allow room to continue round on the arc.

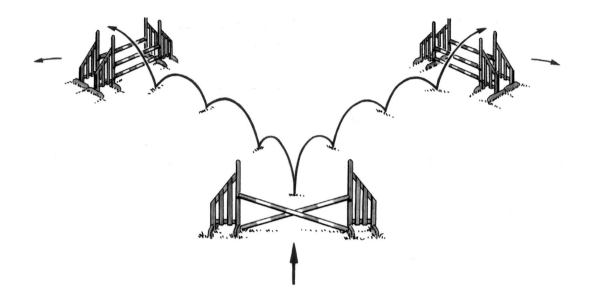

Exercise benefits

- To increase lateral suppleness.

- To ensure equality of balance.

- To improve rideability.

- To promote forward preparation.

Points of awareness

- Approach the cross-pole in a balanced rising trot.

- Focus your attention on either the left or right oxer at your predetermined discretion.

- On landing, continue in canter to the oxer.

- Apply the correct aids to establish the canter lead needed on landing over the cross-pole to bring you directly to your chosen oxer on the desired lead, i.e. eyes ahead, opening inside rein and weight distribution to the inner stirrup.

- If the desired lead is not achieved continue to the fence in canter, jump and carry on in the same direction as your approach. This will encourage the horse to listen to your guidance more carefully on the next attempt, especially if he has found the approach to the oxer awkward off the wrong lead.

- Don't stop between the cross-pole and the oxer. This is simply avoiding the problem and will lead to non-achieving. Continuing on will sharpen both horse and rider reaction.

- Make the horse ambidextrous by ensuring ease to both directions.

- Always approach the cross-pole straight and in trot.

- Don't ride straight between the cross-pole and the oxer, but bend the horse softly on a gentle arc towards the jump. Continue on the same arc after the jump.

- Always jump the middle of both the cross-pole and the oxer.

TRAINING EXERCISE 7

CROSS-POLE WITH LOW RAIL BEHIND

Equipment
4 jump stands
3 poles

Exercise construction
Construct a steep cross-pole by moving the wings a little closer together than normal and placing the top of the crossed rails on the highest hole. The top vee of the cross needs to be reasonably narrow and high.

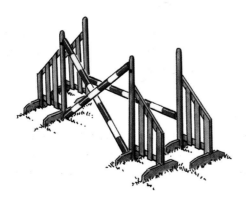

This photo is showing an effective use of the tall cross-pole with a low rail behind. While the horse's forearm is well tucked, his back legs have already left the ground and his head and neck are well extended.

Make an oxer, by adding a single straight bar behind the cross at a height of about half that of the middle of the cross. The width from the cross will be determined by the experience of the horse.

Exercise benefits

- To improve the horse's jumping technique, particularly the hind legs but also the neck, back, shoulders and knees.

Points of awareness

- The horse should be ridden in a positive, forward canter stride to the base of the fence. Try not to stand off or the effectiveness of the exercise will be lost.

- Ensure that the horse has sufficient energy to jump the fence easily from his rhythm. Ensure a closed leg on take-off to maintain impulsion.

- The horse will be required to lift his knees and shoulders first by the tightness and height of the cross. It will then be necessary for him to bring his forearm forward to reach out for the spread.

- Because the rail behind is not high the horse can begin his preparation for landing over the rail. He will be required to lift his hind legs quickly and high to avoid hitting the tall cross, and will be encouraged to pay particular attention to the second half of his bascule. He should be discouraged from cramping his back legs forward towards his belly because of the fence construction, but should find confidence in trailing his hind legs out and up as he completes the landing on his forelegs with a lowered neck.

- Be sure to allow a generous crest release. Do not impede the horse's progress by restricting him with the reins.

- This exercise will require independence of balance from the rider. A well-positioned lower leg giving base support, with your weight into your heel to remain secure, is needed. Keep your eyes up.

- On landing, canter forward, away from the fence, particularly if there has been any loss of forward momentum during the jump.

- If a softer jump is achieved by the horse, with improvement shown in his technique, be quick to reward him. Understanding correctness and achievement should be made clear to the horse to encourage confidence and willingness.

TRAINING EXERCISE 8

GYMNASTIC GRID (1)

Equipment
12 jump wings
12 rails

Exercise construction
A single trot pole is placed on the ground 9 feet (2.7m) in front of a simple cross-pole. At 10 feet 6 inches (3.1m), to create a bounce, a vertical with a ground rail is then followed a stride later (17 feet/5.1m) by a second bounce of verticals, 11 feet (3.3m) apart. Two strides later, to complete the grid, is a parallel.

The heights can be set according to the horse's ability and confidence. Be gradual when making any increase in height, and do not exceed heights that prevent maintenance of a consistent rhythm throughout the exercise. Do not overface your horse.

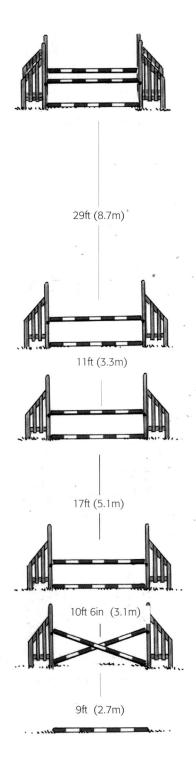

29ft (8.7m)

11ft (3.3m)

17ft (5.1m)

10ft 6in (3.1m)

9ft (2.7m)

Exercise benefits

- To increase athleticism.

- To gain control.

- To encourage improved jumping technique.

- To establish rhythm and constant pace.

- To ensure straightness.

- To improve rider balance.

Points of awareness

- The approach should be made in a controlled rising trot.

- The rider should allow the fences to slow the horse down or encourage him to back off, by being generous with his hand contact throughout.

- The distances are deliberately short to make the horse work harder to collect his balance and stride, and to encourage self-preservation and a careful attitude.

- An even leg pressure should be maintained by the rider to ensure that the horse's forward rhythm and impulsion do not decrease during the exercise.

- The rider should remain still and independently balanced on his stirrups throughout the exercise. He should allow the horse to jump up through his back by remaining light; he should neither get ahead of the movement nor be left behind.

- If the rider pushes his shoulders forward when jumping it will not assist the horse to come back off the fence when making his bascule.

- Go straight – the cross bar at the beginning is designed to centre the start of the exercise. Further cross-bars could be constructed at any point during the exercise.

- Always canter away from the grid and do not let the horse fall behind the leg into trot. Make an effective downward transition.

TRAINING EXERCISE 9

GYMNASTIC GRID (2)

Equipment
14 jump wings
14 poles

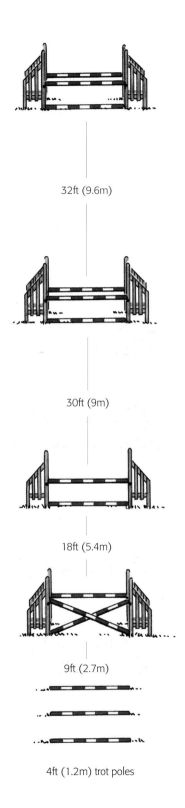

32ft (9.6m)

30ft (9m)

18ft (5.4m)

9ft (2.7m)

4ft (1.2m) trot poles

Exercise construction
Three trot poles are placed 4 feet (1.2m) apart before an oxer with the front constructed as a cross-pole. There is 9 feet (2.7m) from the last trot pole to the base of the cross; 18 feet (5.4m) further on is a vertical, then 30 feet (9m) to an oxer, and another 32 feet (9.6m) to a final oxer.

Exercise benefits

• To ensure the horse is in front of or responsive to the rider's leg.

• To encourage extension of the horse's stride.

• To establish a forward, open jump.

Points of awareness

• The three trot poles will help the horse to remain in balance as the rider begins to ride forward to approach the initial oxer.

• Care should be taken not to push the horse out of his rhythm as the stride is lengthened and the energy levels increased towards the fence.

• The rider should not drop the horse or allow him to become disengaged over the trot poles.

• Impulsion (contained energy) should be maintained.

• The horse should be encouraged to take the rein forward and not down.

• The rider should close the leg and encourage the horse

forward down the line. The energy and length of the stride should be created from the rider's leg, not from his seat. Sitting heavy and pushing with the seat will only encourage the horse to hollow and possibly quicken, rather than lengthen.

- Use generous ground lines at the fences to allow the horse to stay confidently moving forward. By bringing the ground rail out in front of the top rail slightly, the profile of the fence will be softened and become less demanding.

- Canter positively away from the last element.

This rider is encouraging her horse to extend his stride while negotiating a grid. Greater effect would be achieved if she had a stronger leg position, with more weight in the heel. A lighter seat would allow the horse to round his back and produce a longer stride.

TRAINING EXERCISE 10

IMPROVING THE CANTER

Equipment
3 poles

Exercise construction
Place the poles on the ground in a straight line at pre-specified distances. The example illustrated shows 64 feet (19.2m) between poles 1 and 2 and 40 feet (12m) between poles 2 and 3. This represents a distance suitable for a normal

five strides between poles 1 and 2, and three strides between poles 2 and 3.

The poles could be altered to suit any number of strides between, based on one non-jumping stride equalling 12 feet (3.6m). Allow 2 feet (30cm) either side of the pole for stepping over the pole – you are not jumping.

It is more useful to use several strides in preference to few.

Exercise benefits

- To establish rhythm, balance and control.

- To encourage straightness.

- To improve the engagement of the canter.

Points of awareness

- The exercise should be completed entirely in canter.

- The speed should remain constant throughout.

- The rhythm should not be altered by the influence of the poles. Excessive jumping or rushing should be discouraged.

Poles on the ground can be useful in improving the horse's balance and rhythm in canter. They can also assist in developing elasticity within the stride.

5 strides then 3 strides

6 strides then 4 strides

7 strides then 5 strides

64ft (19.2m) ———— ———— 40ft (12m) ————

- Straightness should be maintained over the poles and travelling between.

- Each stride should be regular in size. Once the required stride pattern is consistently achieved through the establishment of a correct balance, rhythm, and level of control, the horse can be asked to further engage his canter stride to complete an additional stride between each pole.

- The horse should not become heavier but should come lighter in the forehand while distributing more weight on his hindquarters. He should not lose his quarters to either side.

- Once the additional stride is completed successfully, he can be asked to execute yet another stride between each pole. He is required to shorten his frame and stride even further whilst engaging his hocks. His response to the increased demands should be increased activity of his hind legs and not a reduction.

- If the horse falls into trot, simply re-attempt, increasing the application of the lower leg to encourage greater activity.

- Be gradual and realistic in your demands. The further apart the poles are placed initially, the greater the number of additional strides that are likely to be achieved.

- Consider the exercise to be about cantering and not jumping, but stay light with your seat to allow the horse freedom through his back. Stay upright with your upper body as the strides shorten, to remain distributed over the horse's centre of balance.

- For successful cross-country riding, the rider must have the confidence that he can perform three quite obviously different canters within the pace itself, i.e. three gears. What these 'gears' are called is irrelevant, although they are mostly described as collected, working, and extended. When I am teaching I often refer to them as 'sneaking about', 'ordinary' and 'going places'. This exercise should assist in achieving this goal and preventing you from falling into the trap of possessing only one type of canter.

- The exercise can prove useful for developing the rider's ability to count strides and recognise distance.

TRAINING EXERCISE 11

STRAIGHTNESS

Equipment
2 jump wings
2 poles with painted stripes
1 ground pole

Exercise construction
Construct a regular vertical fence with a solid ground line. The height is of little consequence.

Exercise benefits

- To establish straightness

- To gain control and improve rideability

- To prepare for arrowheads and corners without using a narrow-faced obstacle.

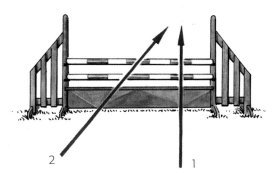

Points of awareness

- Before approaching the fence in canter, select a designated spot on the jump over which you wish to pass. This could be a specific ring of coloured paint, etc.

- The chosen route need not necessarily be in the centre of the fence. It may be to the left or the right of middle (see diagram, line 1).

- Approach the desired spot on a straight line and ensure that the direction is maintained over the fence and continued while departing the jump.

- Any sideways movement should become immediately apparent to the rider or an observer.

- Keeping your eyes focused above and beyond your chosen spot will help you feel any drifting effects or directional changes.

- Ensure that the horse's stride is sufficiently collected to allow the required accuracy and control.

- Remember that in order to ride straight it is important to ride forward. Don't pull against the horse on the approach to the fence or you may create crookedness.

- A straight line can also be practised on a diagonal over the fence off either rein. (See diagram, line 2.) Again, no variation of direction should be evident throughout the exercise.

- On the diagonal, it will become easier for the horse to drift sideways as the jump runs away from him. A constant, equal contact of both hands and legs will channel his motion straight.

- Be sure that you remain straight in the saddle.

TRAINING EXERCISE 12

DIAGONAL LINES

Equipment
Sufficient materials to build 3 oxer jumps and 2 verticals

Exercise construction
First build a single oxer on the centre line of your jumping arena half way from each end. The fence should be set at a comfortable height for the horse's level of training and experience.

On a diagonal line which will dissect the initial oxer, build two further oxers on an even three-stride distance. On the opposite diagonal line build two vertical fences, also on three even strides.

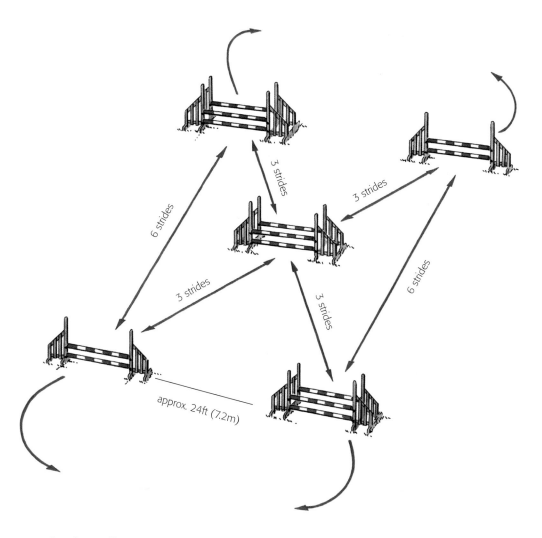

3 strides

6 strides

3 strides

3 strides

3 strides

6 strides

approx. 24ft (7.2m)

Exercise benefits

- To develop straightness/correct crookedness.

- To encourage forward thinking and riding.

- To establish rhythm.

- To improve manoeuvrability.

Points of awareness

- The objective of the exercise is to ride a direct, straight line between all three elements of the diagonal sequence of fences.

- Try to keep an even stride length throughout, with regularity of pace.

- The rider must focus his eyes ahead on the fences throughout to highlight any deviation of line at the earliest instance.

- Take care not to drift off line over the jumps themselves. Dissect the jumps on an angle without allowing the fence to influence your straight line.

- Establish the correct line early to ensure straightness throughout the entire sequence. Do not rush your presentation to the first fence. It may be prudent to attempt the diagonal that involves the two verticals before attempting the line of oxers.

- The benefit of using an oxer as the middle fence of the sequence is to encourage positive forward riding.

TRAINING EXERCISE 13

ESTABLISHING RHYTHM AND COUNTING STRIDES

Equipment
2 wings
4 poles

Exercise construction
Build a simple vertical fence on the centre line of your jumping arena, at an equal distance from both ends..

Ensure that there is a solid ground rail on each side of the fence to enable an approach to be made from both directions.

The fence does not need to be very high.

Exercise benefits

- To establish a balanced rhythm.

- To educate the rider to evaluate distance.

- To promote rideability, control and continuity.

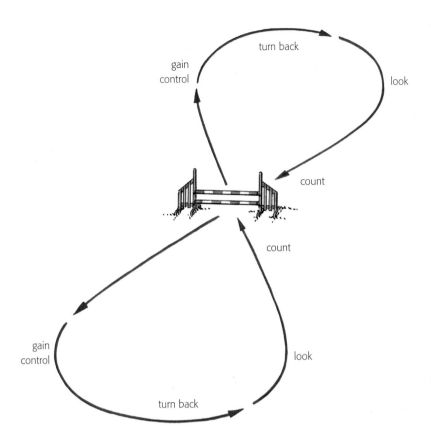

Points of awareness

• The exercise should be carried out in a balanced and controlled canter throughout. Using the fence as cross-over point, a figure of eight should be ridden continuously. To encourage flow and rhythm it is desirable to execute a change of lead over the jump. If not achieved, the lead leg issue should be ignored in the interests of maintaining the canter.

• Once the desired line has been established, the rider should endeavour to count the last stride before take-off, calling 'one' aloud. On returning to the fence the last two strides should be counted, i.e. 'one, two'. On the next approach, the last three strides are counted: 'one, two, three', followed by four, and so on.

• It may be difficult for an inexperienced rider to develop an eye for distance much beyond five or six strides, and it may indeed take considerable time and practice before judgment is confirmed.

• It is important to maintain continuity throughout the exercise to assist rider education. Think ahead, flow around the turns to allow sufficient room to keep a constant speed and stride pattern.

• By counting out loud, any variation in the rhythm on approach to the fence should become immediately obvious as the counting will quicken if the horse speeds up. An observer on the ground would be useful and should add to the fun!

• Do not be hurried.

• Maintain rhythm after the jump, connect the canter at all times, gain control before making your turn, and look back at the fence early in the turn to ensure advance preparation.

TRAINING EXERCISE 14

TROT CROSS-POLES – VERTICAL AND OXER

Equipment
6 wings
8 poles

Exercise construction

Build a single cross-pole and an oxer of cross-poles side by side. Place a single trot pole on the take-off and landing sides of each fence.

For the single cross-pole, use a distance between the fence and the ground poles of only 8ft 6ins (2.5m).

For the oxer of cross-poles, use a distance of 10ft 6ins (3.1m).

Exercise benefits

• To establish rhythm and control.

• To build power and impulsion.

• To promote rideability.

• To encourage rider independence and skills.

Points of awareness

- The rider should alternate his approach between the two fences.

- The horse should remain in trot in his approach to both fences, right up until the point of take-off. He must not speed up, slow down or break into canter.

- The rider should remain rising to help maintain a rhythmic trot. Rising will assist the rider in distributing his weight onto his stirrups, so helping him to achieve independent balance during the exercise.

- The horse should take off and land inside the trot poles placed on the ground at both fences.

- The approach should be made off each rein and equally from either direction.

- At the vertical cross-pole the horse should be retained in a shortened frame and with a collected stride. The rider must ensure that his elbows are bent and elastic, to discourage resistance. He should not fix his hands and stiffen his arms. The horse's bascule should be short and high with the rider keeping a 'feel' on the horse's mouth. The impression should be of connection, control and regulation.

- At the oxer of cross-poles, the approach should be more forward. The stride and horse's frame should be extended within the trot rhythm. The impres-

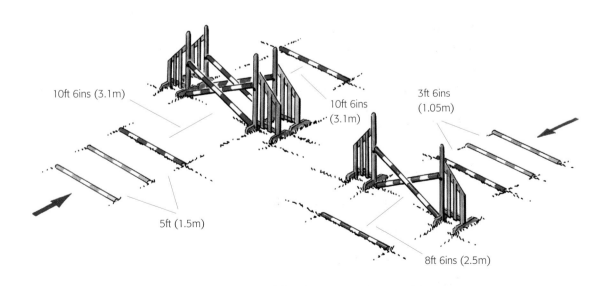

10ft 6ins (3.1m)

10ft 6ins (3.1m)

3ft 6ins (1.05m)

5ft (1.5m)

8ft 6ins (2.5m)

sion should now be of power and of impulsion. (The horse can now go away from the fence in canter.)

- Both jumps should be executed easily within the rhythm.

- Additional trot poles could be used on the approach to maintain rhythm and balance if necessary – close together when engaging the trot, more distance when lengthening the trot (see diagram).

- The rider must remain in balance with the horse. Look up, not down. Do not get ahead of the movement or be left behind.

Index